D1592524

FAILING GOD

Five steps to failing better

K.E. MACPHIE

Shell —

Thanks for inspiring

me to keep failing good

♡ Kirsten

GRATITUDE

As I have learned to come from a place of gratitude, I am especially grateful for those who helped inspire me to write this book, whether they knew it or not.

I am deeply grateful to the nonfiction authors I clung to as I climbed out of my depression: Simon Sinek, Michael Hyatt, Dave Ramsey, Jen Sincero, Marie Kondo, Dan Harris, Benjamin Hoff, Robert Pirsig, Angela Duckworth, and Brené Brown. Thanks for saving me.

To my editor, Regina Lifrieri, who not only made my book technically better but also cheer leaded me as my target audience and the wonderful type of woman I hope finds support in this book.

To my friends, for reading the blog that started this all, giving feedback on posts and ideas, and letting me spitball over dinners or drives for the last four years.

To my dad, Rich, for staying creative and dreaming big. He wrote a book long before I did, and something about him just doing it told me I had it in me to do it, too.

To my sister, Heather, for just existing as a positive person and opening the world of self-help authors to me, and I am so grateful they were there when I needed them.

To my sister, Shannon, for reminding me that I can do whatever I want and for living that example.

To my mom, Breta, for supporting me in every way whenever I needed it, from the time it was just the two of us through helping me make my dreams come true, I'll like you forever, love you for always!

To Lumberjack, for all the lessons you have taught me - from how to ice fish to how to love myself. And for seeing my beauty and brilliance so confidently that I could finally see it for myself. Thank you for being by my side through some of my biggest transformations, the least of which is through authoring this book.

To my greatest successes, my Tiny Giants, Colton and Michael, whom I hope I have raised to try and to fail better; to become even bolder and braver than I will ever be.

And thank you, Reader, for giving this time to me.

TABLE OF CONTENTS

K.E. MACPHIE

I am Here to Help

Who am I?

I am a Myers-Briggs ENFJ: A devoted altruist.

I am Enneagram 2: The Helper.

I am an astrological Libra: Constantly searching for peace and balance in a chaotic world.

I am a Big Five high in agreeableness, conscientiousness, and openness.

I am a military Veteran, enlisted Army medic.

I am a graduate with a master's in public health.

I am a member of the Leech Lake Band of Ojibwe.

I am a violence preventionist for the military.

I am an author of self-help blogs and books (now).

I am a mother, a sister, a daughter, a partner, a friend.

At my deepest core, I am someone who wants to give all of myself to help the world however I can.

What am I doing here?

Within these pages, I share some of my biggest failures to help others survive—and thrive—in their own lives. Several years ago, this book began as a blog. My friends and family would read and respond to my posts with genuine support and an appreciation that I allowed myself to be open and vulnerable about issues they had secretly faced. While I continued writing to reach others and offer guidance through my own experiences, I couldn't figure out what I ultimately wanted to do with the content. However, after a significant amount of effort invested in learning about myself through personality tests, therapy, and self-reflection, I realized that what I really wanted to do was to help others. I'm not here to change my life, I want to change yours. I'm here for even one person who Googles "failure" in the depths of their darkest time and finds someone who has been in the same pit of despair but can offer a map out of the darkness.

My educational background is in public health, or healing populations of people in various sectors. Over the course of my career, I have focused more closely on military mental health. I started as an Army medic, but thanks to achieving my master's degree through benefits associated with the GI Bill, I transitioned to a focus on substance abuse prevention, suicide awareness, and family support, currently working in family violence and abuse prevention. Working in all these different areas has put me face-to-face with people who feel like they are failing in life—with addiction, depression, financially, professionally, or emotionally. I'm here to tell anyone reading these words that failure is not the end but rather a part of life, and I've seen people come back, I've helped them get there, I did it myself, you can do it, too.

Where do I hope you go with this?

I hope this book pushes you forward through your inevitable failures a little better. It's a culmination of all the lessons I've learned and observed compiled in one place to, hopefully, make the journey to betterment a little easier than I've had it. Learn from my mistakes, but also be brave enough to get out there and make some of your own.

When should you read this?

If you are hesitant about taking your next big step, you need to feel confident that failure won't crush your world, I want to help you try it, even if you fail it. If you are wrapped in a cocoon of blankets or ignoring friends' phone calls because you've already failed, I want to help you feel it and fix it. If a lingering failure is holding you back from your potential, I want to help you process it and grow.

There is a way to fail better, and maybe you've experienced it and tuned into how to bounce back in your own past, but I hope you can read this and know that whatever you're going to try, you might fail, but you can fail better than before.

Why am I qualified to be an expert on failure?

It's not my college degree or my middle-aged wisdom that gives me credibility. As you will read, I have lived through some massive fails and I'm still here. I've taken my own advice of not just failing and quitting but I've been curious about myself and about human nature, which has driven me to take the time to evaluate why and how these things happened and how I can be better. I don't think I'm perfect, I don't think my life has hit its potential, but I think I have a lot to share about what I've learned, and I want to collect all of my thoughts and lessons into one place: this book.

How do you fail better?

Try it – be brave and go do the things that scare you.

Fail it – take your hits as part of the course.

Feel it – take inventory of the emotions as they come.

Fix it – either adjust your course or take a new path.

Grow – move forward with all the lessons and learning along the way.

That's it! Now keep reading to see how I applied that theory to the failures that have defined my first thirty-seven years of doing life.

STEP 1: TRY IT

K.E. MACPHIE

The Fail: I Lost an Election

Losing an election wasn't one single failure. The overall feeling was one of experiencing several different failures all at the same time.

It was a public humiliation because everyone knew my dreams and became well aware that I wasn't achieving them. Hiding behind the curated social media frame of life successes simply wasn't an option.

It was a career failure, as the trajectory of my job title and earning potential in public service I had envisioned for the majority of my adult life faded away.

It was an avocational failure for someone who made politics such an integral life component. My friends, social life, and overall enjoyment were based on community and political involvement, which died with the loss.

It was a relational failure, as I realized that the voting public and community to which I had devoted countless volunteer hours and shown fierce commitment just…weren't that into me.

It was, as my friend called it, a load-bearing failure—a failure that was decades in the making that crushed me in a single day.

If you had asked me what my life plan was in the spring of 2004, a bright-eyed, optimistic, eighteen-year-old, I'd have told you my plans to do the military thing for a bit, then start college with a Poli-Sci major at the U after training, while acting as a Congressional intern in DC during the summers. I knew all about the crazy hours and cramped living, how the job entailed little more than running errands for people who made more money in an hour than I would in a week, and still, I remained excited to be an intern. I couldn't wait to be there because I knew it would give me the experience and clout to advance and run for bigger things.

I made it through part of my first semester at the University of Minnesota before a surprise baby, and the resulting shotgun wedding rerouted me through my twenties. But, even living with two little kids and an Iraq War Veteran, I stayed involved in community projects and met influential people. Eventually, at age thirty, I was asked to run for office. Just like that, I felt my dreams were back on track. No Poli-Sci major, no internship, but years of life experience in its place.

In 2016, during my first run, I was just a name on a ballot. I had signed up as a candidate but learned two months into my election run that I wasn't allowed to campaign because of who my employer was. In actuality, I hadn't made any real plans to win because of where I was in life at the time. It was all fun, and I wasn't particularly disappointed to lose 42-57 for the role of State Senator. Instead, I was thrilled with how much I learned behind the scenes, and I was well aware that people would know my name next time. I carefully observed the entire process, took notes on what I would do when I *really* ran, and formed relationships and connections to have people ready to back me when that day arrived.

When my party suggested I run for State Representative in 2018, I went all in. I cleared it with work, consulted my kids, and ran exactly how I wanted—on my terms—and I ran to win. From July 1 until November 6, I campaigned hard every single day for my community and my party. I volunteered at events, sat in on board meetings, went door-to-door, walked in parades, patronized local businesses on Small Business Saturdays, talked, listened, and did everything I thought I was supposed to in order to be successful in politics. I truly believed I could win.

Then I didn't. Surprisingly, I lost by a bigger margin than when I did absolutely nothing in 2016.

I discovered I had lost while in the bar bathroom during my victory party. I was spending election night with a small sample of dedicated friends and family who supported me over the past several months. I had been taking the "whatever happens, it was meant to be" approach—the high road—and just trying to be present and enjoy the night. However, insecurity crept into my curiosity, and I snuck away to check on the results alone in a handicapped stall across the building. I lost. More accurately, I lost by so much in 6 out of 7 districts that even if I had swept the last one, I wouldn't have come up enough to win. While almost 6,000 people voted for me, twice that number voted for him. I returned to the group, some of whom had also checked the results while I stepped out, and I was welcomed back to "We'll get 'em next time" encouragement and "Fuck 'em, let's get drunk" solidarity. I smiled and agreed. I didn't cry. I just slowed down the night, packed up all the extra food, and left alone.

I stopped by my party's gathering, where the mood was just as destitute as I felt. I checked in with friends while my mom took the kids home and put them to bed. I didn't want to walk in my front door until I was sure I had covered all my bases and that no one would greet me inside.

I finally returned home at around midnight—
and then, I cried. No, not cried... sobbed. I sobbed
harder than I had in years, a heaving,
hyperventilating, screaming, eye-stinging, tears in the
dark, alone in my room, sob fest. Five months of
exhaustion and stress and every emotion I had felt
during that time came out at once, and I felt them all.
Soon, a friend called to check on me and brought the
hysterical crying down to mere sniffling. I don't
remember ever completely stopping. My eyes just
finally shut because they hurt so badly.

On November 7, I woke up and cried again.
This time, silently and through a throbbing headache
that came on the moment I remembered the day
before, like a bad hangover of cringe-worthy regret. I
started my day and got my kids ready for school,
crying in the car as I drove past the campaign yard
signs, now nothing more than a cruel taunt with my
name printed clearly on each. I cried, staring blankly
at my computer after any of my wonderfully
supportive co-workers came to offer condolences, and
even when my puppy peeked out from under my
desk, clearly trying to cheer me up. I cried again on
my way home, listening to Adele, and trying to
squeeze all the tears out so I could wipe my eyes in
the driveway. I did not want to let my kids see how
sad I was. I cried at my night job when my apolitical
bartender friend asked how I did and gave me a hug,
only then realizing I was completely unable to talk
about it without sobbing. I cried for days in what felt
like a constant stream of tears.

Then, after the days passed, I cried for a week. I stopped replying to people who asked how I was because there was nothing to say. Ten days later, the arbitrary deadline I had given myself to stop being sad came and went—so I cried about that. I stopped drinking (after ONLY drinking for a significant period) because I knew I had hit rock bottom in self-pity, resentment, and depression only grew louder after a few (or 7-10) beers. Without alcohol to buffer the pain of conversation, I stopped going out because I didn't like being caught off guard by friends or acquaintances and crying in public. I even cried at Thanksgiving when a family member asked about the race, and I couldn't even fake that I was totally over it.

Two months after election day, I attempted to attend a political meeting with a friend. It was meant to be my return to the community scene with her by my side. I drove to the spot with knots in my stomach but proud that I had managed to pull myself back up. On the way, I turned on my hype playlist to help me get out of my head. I walked in the door and waved to my friend, but I also saw people who had won their races, people who had rooted against me, and many who had said ugly things about me in the political arena and who were now feigning pity over my loss through joy at their gain. My throat got tight soon after I arrived, and I went to the bathroom to get the tears out. They wouldn't stop for five full minutes. I looked in the mirror and told myself to get it together, but I physically could not stop crying. So, I hustled out with my head down, quickly grabbed my things, apologized to my friend, and left.

I didn't like this version of myself, but I was incapable of being anything else. From that moment, my agoraphobia grew, as did my disdain for my community who didn't vote for me, my friends who didn't help enough and who supported a loser, and myself for being stupid enough to think I could win. I grew increasingly isolated and bitter, only leaving my house for work or my kids. I slept a lot, made excuses to cancel plans, quit existing commitments, and ignored many of the most important aspects of my life because staying involved hurt too much.

I had failed not only in the election but also at being a gracious loser and a resilient community member, and—truth be told—I was failing as a functioning human being. I was becoming completely defined by one failure, causing the dominoes to fall, leading me to fail in everything else.

K.E. MACPHIE

The Lesson: Failing Good Requires Five Steps

Try it. Fail it. Feel it. Fix it. Grow.

Around New Year's 2019, I hit the bottom of the pit of self-pity and failure. While everyone was making resolutions and looking forward to a clean slate, I couldn't even see a starting point from which to move forward. Fortunately, I realized I had become an expert on failure—and I knew I could use that to my advantage and to help others.

After this, my biggest and most public failure, I had to do my own research and put in the work to pull myself out of the resulting hole of despair in which I found myself. It took a great deal of help, which came scattered from a variety of different people and sources, some less expected than others. Now that I have finally found myself standing on the outside looking in with 20/20 vision, I want to reach my hand in to guide you out, too. I'll cite experts, tell

22

terribly embarrassing personal stories, and enlighten you with perspectives I haven't even shared with my best friends or family. I'll dig my heels in to pull you out of your pit, because I promise the view is much better out here.

A lot of climbing out of my pit has been about taking baby steps forward, sometimes slow and sometimes quick, trying to get out of my own way. But the most important part is to give yourself patience and grace to take the time you need to stand up and start stepping. While the titles of the steps may seem broad, I promise that within those wide brush strokes, you will find a series of small motivational wins and valuable guidance. I want to put forth a clear GPS to success for you—one I wish someone had given me when I hit my own personal rock bottom. There was a well-thought-out reason for the order of steps and the reason to work them all the way through, that I want to briefly address up front.

Try It sounds obvious, but in a culture where 31% of adults suffer from anxiety, it's harder to do things that don't offer us certain outcomes. But ask any hospice nurse, and they will tell you that the most common deathbed regret is dreams that have gone unfulfilled. Very rarely will people regret something they tried and failed; they regret not trying at all. You'll never feel completely confident or totally ready, so I'll encourage you to try it anyway. Try it with the pit in your stomach and the hesitation in your heart. It won't feel like a success if you never failed at something you always wanted to try.

Fail It is exactly what this is all about. Fall on your face. Find the limit. Really crash and acknowledge it without excuses or trying to sweep the devastation under the proverbial rug. Some people hang in the failure and keep trying to justify why it's not, or maybe they never admit how hard they tried and how painful the failure was. Just be honest to yourself, even if you still can't admit it to anyone else, so you can move on to the next step. You can try to fix it right away, but don't skip the next step, you have to do it in order.

Feel It is what this world needs more of. The toxic positivity and empty advice that tells you to bounce back glosses over how you do that. You do it by feeling. Fall down, and pout for a minute. Rub the spots where it's sore or treat the injuries of the fall before you get up to do it again. Feel it with honesty and depth, not just platitudes and false expectations. But then, don't feel it forever. Give the feelings space, but also hold them loosely and let them go. Staying too long can weigh you into depression, but need to keep in perspective that you can move on in healing with some pragmatism and analysis as we go to the next step.

Fix It can go two ways: change it and try again or check it off and adjust course to something totally new. Either way, you're looking back at the failure, having felt all the emotions of it, you need to be honest with yourself about if this is something you can fix enough to try again, or if the fix means fixing your sights on something else. Either way is ok.

24

Despite what your coach said, quitters can prosper in other areas of life, even if they don't win this one game.

Grow is such a lovely and calm place to be. Once you've attempted the thing – with all the butterflies in your stomach – and fell on your face, you took time to grieve the loss, no matter how big or small; you took the thought to critically evaluate what went wrong and how you can improve in your next step; and now, with all the new wisdom that only comes with experience, you can grow. And the next thing you try can be bigger or better or both. This is how we evolve. And sharing our evolutions is how we bring up society along with us.

When we talk about failure herein, we are discussing only the things we actually attempt. To fail, we have to have a dream, make a goal, create a plan, take steps toward achieving it, and somehow still fall short. We can fail for a hundred different reasons. Sometimes, you just run out of steam. Sometimes, other people really do get in the way, and you have to adjust. Sometimes circumstances change, and those things that seemed quite possible at the planning stage become impossible later. Sometimes, the objective just wasn't meant for you, and you need to accept it.

Another basic qualifier of failure I want to outline is that there are smarter ways to fail—and many failures are worthwhile and come with valuable lessons and insights. Take my election loss, for example. Rather than run for a local election, I could have quit my job and uprooted my family to move to Washington, DC, which I couldn't afford, to force my way into politics, and likely fail there. I could have run for President, given that it had been my ultimate goal. But I didn't do that. Instead, I took smaller, less invasive steps to see if it was even the direction I wanted to go. And, as it turned out—it wasn't. I got to learn that with a lesser financial or lifestyle punch than if I had uprooted to DC. That's failing better.

Knowing what I do now, I am grateful for that failure. I am so glad I failed locally and that, even though my original path to election didn't work, I forged one anyway. I put forth enough effort and experience to check the box off and leave feeling like I tried enough to avoid the deathbed regret. I will always know just how hard I wanted it because I witnessed the extent of the hurt that came when I missed.

I read a lot of motivational literature on my way out of the pit. Many authors wrote about the importance of visualizations and ideas, such as, "If you can dream it, you can achieve it!" Of course, this may sound like incredibly inspiring cheerleading from an outsider's perspective, but reading it from the dark, desolate depths of the pit after a life-numbing failure SUCKS. I saw my dreams before my eyes and did everything in my power to achieve them, yet I still didn't "achieve it." Under those circumstances, that advice is like pouring lemon in a cut while the wound is still wide open.

It wasn't until author Simon Sinek, and his more formal and less motivational approach to life improvement, reframed my views with his book, *Start with Why,* that I could see I was still moving toward those dreams—even through my failure. Failing to reach my goal was just an annoying sidetrack; I could still be on the path to my real purpose in life.

I had decided on the thought that my service-oriented heart, the same one that led me to enlist in the military, volunteer at the hospital, and run in the political arena, was destined for elected office. It seemed to make sense. Winning that election would have been my pinnacle, finally satisfying that insatiable need to serve and feel appreciated. It wasn't until the crushing loss and the resulting realization that this dream wouldn't happen that I could see that an election wasn't my ticket out. My "why" for running had been to help improve lives and to do so for as many people as possible.

Serving in the military after 9/11 was my large-scale service, whereas running for office was on a more local scale, but I began to think it through a little further and in a different way: What if I could still reach people but in a different way? What if I could write a book and reach people one by one? Would that work for me? Would it work for them? While you're sitting there, reading or listening to me, consider the idea that we are having a personal heart-to-heart chat with the goal of improving your singular life. What if I could have those one-on-ones with thousands of people at once? Maybe this was how I was meant to serve. And if that doesn't work, maybe there's still another way. And perhaps there is no pinnacle, but instead an ongoing, continuous, and evolving service to others which provides contentment throughout the endeavor. I would love to see this book made into motivational speeches like Brené Brown's, viral videos like Simon Sinek's, or a radio show like Dave Ramsey's. Maybe it could become a movie or a movement. It will be whatever it needs to be, but I will be happy to have merely planted the seed and let it grow in you.

So, let's get back to our focus on how to fail and, more specifically, how to try. To fail successfully, you must aim for something to care about achieving. I find inspiration from SAMHSA's eight dimensions of wellness, which are:

Emotional

Spiritual

Intellectual

Physical

Environmental

Financial

Occupational

Social

And don't just select a single area of focus for your life improvement, work on them all at once. Some think you can only succeed at one thing at a time, but I think that the "one thing" you are aiming toward should be your general overall peace and wellness. The dimensions are all ingredients in that. There's an intelligent way to do this, but we'll get to that in the FIX IT section of this book. Right now, just know there is a pathway out when you're ready, keep the steps in order.

While at the bottom of the pit, reclusive from my friends and family, I created an Eight Dimensions vision board with goals for the year, plus one made up of goals for my children. I wrote each goal, cut and pasted pictures from the internet alongside them, and posted them in my bedroom directly in front of my bed. It was the first thing I saw in the morning, so I had to look at it anytime I left my safe space. It acted as a GPS for where I was headed which, at the time, was out of the pit. If I realized I was bored or had a free hour, I looked to my board to see what needed some work today. Then, I'd call a friend, read a book, or meditate for 20 minutes. It could be something I could do quick, or start long-term, but that would progress me toward success in one of the nine areas.

Each wellness area was given a present-tense statement of success and several tiny goals for how to get there. The biggest key to sticking with my board was a deep search for the "why" behind my goals.

Why do I want to lose weight? The easy answer is to look hot and feel better. But what would I do with that improved look and feel? I'd turn it into confidence and energy to increase my capacity to help others and to give some of my energy to them when they're running low.

Why do I want to get out of debt? The easy answer is to have more money. But what I would do with all the money would be to make more significant donations that would make a larger impact, to take care of my children and their children, and to have the money to help others become the best versions of themselves.

Why do I want to write a book? Sure, it would be cool to create a passive income and meet Oprah— but the truth is that I want to reach as many people as possible to help them in the same way so many books helped me when it was getting cold and dark.

These are different goals, but they all have one common thread: I want to be my best self to have the ability to give more of myself to others. That's it. From weight to wealth, it always comes back to the same thing. I often feel like I'm Captain Marvel wearing a limiter that is holding me back from my full potential. I can pull it off by achieving the goals—losing weight, saving money, and doing so many other small things—to make a big difference in my life. Maybe your limiter is your mental health struggle. Maybe it's the people with whom you surround yourself. Maybe you struggle with an addiction consuming your attention, stopping you from moving forward in any other area. But look! Here you are, maybe still in the pit, but willing to look up instead of just being content to sit, head down, curled up in the corner.

My favorite TikTok psychotherapist, Matthias Baker, compared the various areas of self-improvement to making a salad. The big picture is that I want a delicious Cobb salad. However, to get that salad, I require many different ingredients that work together to provide that one big flavor I'm going for. The lettuce, bacon, and avocado might actually be weight loss, financial security, and a good network of friends. When they combine and are all fulfilled effectively, they function to make me into the person I want to be—someone who can serve in any capacity because I have the physical, emotional, and financial requirements necessary to be a helper. That's my salad. That's my big goal.

At eighteen, my reasons for running for office were selfish – I wanted to be rich and famous like many idealistic youths throughout history. As my worldview and wisdom shifted with age and maturity, I saw they were becoming more altruistic and based on meeting other people's needs. However, for months after the election, I was angry that I had even tried. That effort killed a spark in me that was once so optimistic and felt the good would prevail in politics. I still don't have that spark back. I still won't volunteer for anything or door-knock for even the best candidates anymore—and while I do miss that, I have taken the time to feel it and fix it to know it now as a boundary, not just bitterness.

But in exchange for that ending, I feel so open in saying I tried. I know I won't ever wish I could run my best race, because I did. I won't ever have to wonder if I could have won, because I didn't. Questions were answered during the process, and even though it didn't lead to the outcome I had wanted, I have my definitive yeses, and nos. I am more content with that result than spending a lifetime inquiring and regretting the fear that could have stopped me from ever running.

Some politico friends have encouraged me to take part in another election. Many of them lost their first run, too, but won the second or third time around. I, however, feel content and get a great deal of closure in saying that's just not me. I don't have the drive anymore. My dream has taken a new path, and I'm ok with that.

K.E. MACPHIE

The Fail: I Came in Dead Last in a Half Marathon

I hate running. Whenever I run, I distract myself by imagining several different ways I could cause an injury and make it look like an accident to justify quitting. Like, "Oh, there's a pothole! Maybe if I step in it just the wrong way, a twisted ankle will keep me off the road for a while..." It's dark, it's depressing, but it keeps my mind busy, so I guess it works.

Despite my loathe for running, I had no choice but to do it regularly as a member of the military. We were tested on a timed two-mile run at least twice a year, and more often than that, I had to do it for remedial training. So, with very little choice, I learned to tolerate running. In 2010, when I lost a significant amount of weight, I made a habit of running despite my disdain for the activity. With my newfound commitment confidently established, I agreed to join my other Army friends when they decided to sign up for a half marathon in 2012.

I had a training schedule I found online and stuck to it pretty well initially. I ran a few miles each day, shifted back and forth between running for distance and time, and signed up for a few 5K runs in the months leading up to the half marathon in August. The furthest run I completed throughout my training was an 8-mile session during the kids' baseball practice. But once the training schedule started listing two-digit distances, I'd make a host of excuses about how I didn't have time for them, so I'd run half the recommendation, then multiply my time by two to count it as a full ten, eleven, or twelve-mile run. Apparently, that's not how it works in official races.

On the day of the half, we all met at my house and left for the race. We hung around at the starting area and made plans to run the whole thing together. I said early on that I would be okay if they went on without me because I knew I was the slowest of the group. The other girls ran at about my pace, but their husbands agreed to run and cheer them on, whereas mine did not. So, rather than be the 5th wheel, I prefaced the whole thing by stating that I'd rather be a loner. We started together, but by the end of mile one, they broke off and went ahead without me.

I knew I was slow, but I knew I could keep going, so I plodded on at a steady jog through the park reserve and to the freeway soundboards before the first significant hill did me in and slowed me into a walk. At first, I said I'd just walk the hill, then get back to running. I reached the hill's apex, ran, then fell back into a walk a minute later. That interval would continue for the entire second half of the race. I'd walk for longer periods until I saw my cheering family, or a water stop, then I might pick up the pace and run for a minute or two. I figured there had to be other walkers behind me, I knew I had passed at least a couple before that hill, but at about mile nine, the trail biker started riding alongside me, picking up cones as I passed them.

"Do you think you're gonna quit in the next mile or two?" he asked casually, oblivious to how demotivating that question was.

"Nope, I'm gonna keep going until I finish or die."

Sighing, he realized he wasn't going to be done early as he had hoped. "Okay, I'll be here," he replied.

So, we kept going like that, him bantering every once in a while, me walking then running through the residential streets. When we got to the park on the east side, I finally saw another runner just ahead of me for the first time in miles. She was on a similar schedule of walking/running; only she didn't have the trail biker on her heels or the cops pulling out of crosswalk duty as soon as she passed them. I made it my goal to pass her, and I did. Then she passed me. Then I passed her again.

We were both clearly in pain, not well-trained, and pulling an extra twenty pounds around this thirteen-mile race that we clearly didn't want to do anymore. But after our 5th or 6th leapfrog, we decided to support each other instead of competing. We commiserated over our thigh chafing and shin pains, but then we started pushing ourselves to run a little longer, urging each other to make it "just around the next corner" or "over to that tree before we take a break." We didn't talk about our lives at all, and I don't even remember her name. Still, I credit her and my mom, who was enthusiastically driving around the route with my cheering babies, with getting me to the end when the pain was getting bad, and the morale was even worse.

I finished the race forty-five minutes after my Army friends, fifteen minutes before the official race stop time, and just a single step behind my new, equally slow friend. I came in 80th out of 80 runners. There was no crowd at the finish line waiting for my arrival—just my friends, family, and a few leftover bananas and energy bars that hadn't been packed up yet.

It wasn't until a week later when most of the other pains had recovered, that I realized my right leg still hurt pretty bad. I went to the doctor and found that an untreated stress fracture had become a full-on break right up the outside of my leg. He told me in a mild Eastern-European accent, "Maybe running is, uh, not for you. Maybe consider biking or swimming, but not so much running." And with that, he gave me an ugly pneumatic air cast dubbed the Super Boot, and I gave up on pretending I could ever be a runner.

The Lesson: Last Place is Better Than Nothing

I admit I hesitate to refer to this particular outcome as a failure because, after all, I did finish the race. I think my true failure would have been to quit mid-race or to have never done it in the first place—in which case I'd have wondered forever if I could have learned to love running. Regardless, I like to share this story because it has helped several friends get over their nerves before their own marathons, half marathons, 5Ks, and triathlons, and because coming in last still fell short of my goal to finish inconspicuously somewhere in the middle alongside my friends.

If the worst-case scenario of you trying something is that you will fail at it, and even if the second worst thing is to succeed in last place, at least that failure will check a box. You tried, and you

38

failed—and that's okay. If any part of you feels like you'll lay on your deathbed and wonder if you could have succeeded at something, then try it. At least you'll know you tried, regardless of the outcome.

So how do you find all these things you want to try and fail? Start your search by trying a whole bunch of different stuff out. During our childhood, we are encouraged to sample a range of different hobbies and activities and seek out interests. We may have attempted to learn to play an instrument, join a sport, camp with a scout group, or whatever—and we used these activities to figure out what gives us a "spark" and what we wish to continue to pursue. However, this doesn't have to end with childhood. If you've forgotten or have yet to determine what gives you a spark, it's not too late to try again. Get started! Sign up for a bunch of intramural teams, and take a community education class in pottery, ribbon dancing, or whatever. Try something new. Nothing you start has to last forever, but it should last until the end of the commitment. If you sign up for a kickball league and realize at game two that you hate and are bad at kickball, make a joke out of it or use it as an opportunity to make friends—but you're in that activity for the rest of the season. You don't have to sign up next year, but this is about practicing your grit and sticking with something even when it's hard. You can do it.

I, like so many others, walk a very thin line between grit and stubbornness; when does one become the other? I knew early into the race that I would be determined to finish, but it cost me a broken leg. Maybe if I quit at that first hill, I could have kept the lesson, but saved the cast.

I was determined to prove the statistics wrong and stayed married beyond the predicted 5-year lifespan of my courthouse wedding. We should have called it quits four years before we actually did.

I have spent far more than I should have in fixing cars, keeping my house, and clinging to things as they are rather than letting go and starting over. So, is my grit improving my quality of life or holding me back from a different direction I should look toward?

To answer that burning question, I read a book appropriately titled *Grit* by Angela Duckworth, and took the Grit Scale assessment. I scored just above 4 out of 5, or above 70% of American adults. According to Dr. Duckworth, this, combined with my high-average IQ, should have rocketed me to the level of super success. Instead, I was a single mom writing a blog and working two jobs to maintain a middle-class suburban life. My grit and stubbornness, which led me to stay in my job, refuse to move more than a mile from my childhood home, and continue dragging my ex-husband around as a project in codependency, held me back from my potential. With that knowledge, I began to unglue myself from some of it, acknowledging the bad and looking for good—and it took years, but I loosened my grip and only held on to what served me.

Even when we acknowledge that it's time to quit something, questions remain. Do we get back up and try again, or should we move on to something completely different? Before the half marathon, many of my runner friends warned that I'd get hooked and want to take on full marathons on at least an annual basis as they did. That certainly didn't happen, and I'm not mad it didn't. Sure, I spent a bit of time feeling like a failure for not finding that addiction as they had, but after that mini pity party, I felt content to move away from my idolization of being "a runner." Instead, I permitted myself to find activities that better fit my life.

Coming in last was more than mildly embarrassing at the moment. The cheering felt patronizing, the volunteers were waiting to go home, and I wasn't coming in gracefully to the finish line in any sense of the word. I was in pain and tired and, really, quite miserable. However, today, twelve years later, when I mention that I ran a half marathon in casual conversation, the other person typically replies with a very genuine, "Wow! You did? That's so cool!" and it feels good every single time—because I did it. Last or not.

The Fail: I Crashed My Motorcycle

Okay, okay, the chapter title of this adventure in failure makes it sound more scary than downright stupid, but I assure you, it was mostly stupid.

I had wanted to ride a motorcycle from the moment I joined the military. While posted at Ft. Sam Houston, TX, I remember walking to the cafeteria several blocks away. As I neared my destination, I saw the most undeniably badass female Sergeant pull over, park her bike, and confidently walk into one of the medical specialty buildings. She exuded such a get-shit-done energy that I could feel it penetrating across the street—and it sparked a "someday" moment within me.

At that time, I had assumed someday would be when I returned home from training, but then came college, babies, and other priorities that weren't conducive to owning a superfluous death machine as a side toy. So, I let that spark burn out and lived the suburban mom life for a decade.

Then, in the summer of 2018, my friend's husband casually mentioned that he was going to be attending motorcycle classes with a Veterans' discount. There were classes? I pondered. And I get a discount? Deal! I was in. I signed up immediately, expecting to take things slowly. That spark had a whole different plan, though, expanding to ignite a full-on bonfire in me. Slow and steady had gone out the window. With the class one month away, I thought it might be helpful to get some on-road practice time beforehand, so I found a bike with low miles for $900 on Craigslist. It was my impulsive side screeching at maximum volume.

The seller was a 50-something Marine biker sporting a goatee, an American flag bandana, and oil-stained Levi's. When he asked if I wanted to test drive it, I told him I didn't know how to drive one, so I couldn't. With that, he threw told me to hold on tight while he gave me a quick lesson with all the brevity of a high-speed Marine: "Go is here, stop is here and there, and... the rest is self-explanatory."

I thought I had it, so I paid the money and sent him on his way. No more than an hour later (remember, impulsive at max volume), I drove my brand-new-to-me bike, for the first time, to a church parking lot about five blocks away to practice. I made it without incident until I had to turn the corner into the lot. I'm still not exactly sure what I did wrong, but through some combination of pulling the handles too fast while attempting to accelerate through the turn, before I knew it, the bike came out from under me— and I lay bleeding on the ground. My phone had fallen out and was crushed, and my joy had turned to resentment.

I got up, gravel sticking to the open wounds on my left knee, elbow, and wrist, and attempted to lift the mildly mangled bike. I looked around to see if any neighbors or church workers had witnessed the events, but no one had. Since I was in pain, and motorcycles are much heavier to hold and lift from the ground than when resting on two wheels, I struggled to get the bike upright. Then, I struggled to turn it back on since pushing it home seemed altogether too exhausting and embarrassing an option to consider.

As I got the engine running and putted my way towards home (5 miles per hour, no turns), it was the first time I very distinctly recall catching myself thinking with failure foresight: "Today, I'm sad, and I hate motorcycles, and I want to quit. But I bet a year from now, this will be a funny memory and a story I can tell, about a hard lesson learned."

That thought didn't stop me from hiding that same bike in my backyard so no one would ask me about it, almost canceling the classes that eventually gave me my confidence back and crying for as many days as I had to change my bandages about what an idiot I had been.

K.E. MACPHIE

The Lesson: Get Up and Try Again

Today, riding my motorcycle is one of my favorite things to do. Biker friends will easily relate as there is no way to describe the absolute freedom and beauty of riding. I was a skeptic at first, mistakenly believing it would feel basically the same as driving a car with the windows down—but riding isn't just the wind against your body, but the closeness you feel to the things around you. You can smell the weed burning from the next car over. You can feel the temperature drop twenty degrees when you hit the lake effect up north. You can hear people having conversations at bus stops. You begin to realize that there's a whole world out there, with countless interactions happening while we drive, but we're usually so insulated from it that none of it matters. It goes unnoticed. Riding a motorcycle fueled that connection to the world again, opening me up to a whole new perspective and a newfound love, appreciation, and connectedness to the universe.

46

I am well aware that if I had kept my bike hidden away and never tried again, I wouldn't know it. I almost never started, then I almost quit, but now I'm so grateful that I kept with it. It was one thing checked off my bucket list that continues to add significant value to my life every summer.

Some of you are reading this book because you're on the brink of trying something new or challenging, but you're paralyzed by the fear of failure. Fear is a poor use of your imagination. You could be using all that emotion and energy to be excited for the extraordinary potential the future holds. Think of the best-case scenario instead of the worst. Ask yourself: what if it all works out? What if a whole new world opens and I learn a new level of love and life?

Assuming the worst is a protection we put on our hearts. When the bar is so low and we succeed, break even, or just barely make it, we can tell people we did better than we ever expected, impressing them with our level of achievement. However, if we assume the best, and have the highest, loftiest goals to tell people about, then when we do well but don't quite get there, we look like failures. I'm writing to tell you, looking like a failure is still better than never trying and truly feeling like one when the window of opportunity has passed.

Even as I wrote this book (over the course of four years now…), I kept expectations low by telling people that my goal was merely to write it—to finish it. Then, I will feel super accomplished when, just by getting 50,000 random words onto a Google Doc, my friends congratulate me on achieving my goal.

What I haven't told them is my bigger dream. I don't just want to write the book... I want to change lives. I want it to be so good that my publisher offers double the advance for my sequel. I want HBO to reach out to request the license for a show the equivalent of a frumpy frostbite version of *Insecure*. I want people lining up to book me for speaking engagements, presentations, and TED Talks about failure—and all because I wrote a book that perfectly encapsulates the human race's experience while inspiring people to be their best selves. Writing all of that down just gave me butterflies. The thing about the physical feeling of butterflies is that I'm never entirely sure whether it's the beginning of fear or excitement, but something tells me that it's up to me to decide.

Find the things that give you butterflies. If you don't know what it is, try a bunch of stuff until you do. It sounds like a little too much fun, right? It is an effort to exercise those success/failure muscles where it doesn't matter quite so much so that you're strong and ready when it does. Once you learn to fail spectacularly at things that have no consequence to your life, you will learn to show up again, even after the worst failures.

A side bonus to this exercise in seeking out new activities to fail (or succeed!) in is that there is a high possibility that you will find something you actually love doing.

For example: I started playing trivia with a friend who had casually mentioned that her team was looking for another player. After playing for a year, the host mentioned that they were expanding and hiring more hosts at other sites—since I was there, I seized that opportunity. Being hired for the role opened the door to see what it's like to have a job I love, one in which I was free to try, fail, then find my voice and succeed in a controlled public setting. After becoming an excellent host, a woman to inform me that I have an exceptional speaking voice and should be on the radio. This triggered a spark, and it's a path I'm still considering today and utilizing with my audiobook—and all because I tried out playing on a trivia team with a casual friend who needed an extra participant.

So, your goal from this chapter is to take on new activities, practice failure, and learn some stuff. Once you've picked a direction, you lay out your path. You will come up with finish-line goals and markers along the way. Take those things that come as small, easy wins, reward yourself, and keep going. Remember to do it all at once. The key to work-life balance is knowing it is never in balance. There are entire months and years when your kids will need a disproportionate amount of your time and attention. There are times you grind at work, and times your health will demand all your attention. On the path to overall wellness, maybe today, you're really up for that 2-mile run, but tomorrow you don't even want to put on pants. Use that day to read a book or call a friend. Improvement anywhere is better than stagnation toward a single focus.

Remember that failing doesn't have to be a step back from achieving one goal but rather a shift to a new one. By losing the election, I closed the book on my political ambitions but have pivoted to focus on writing and positioning myself as an expert on failure. The best part about trying to become a failure expert is that, even if I fail, it only adds a new line to my resume and expertise!

As Oscar Wilde said, "Experience is the hardest kind of teacher. It gives you the test first and the lesson after." So, with that said, give yourself tests, learn and grow, but… always start by trying.

K.E. MACPHIE

STEP 2: FAIL IT

K.E. MACPHIE

I Failed a Semester of Grad School

I had always been a low-to-mid three-point-something GPA type. I put in enough work to be considered smart but not enough to stress over a B versus an A. That didn't change much as I graduated from a hodgepodge of colleges and entered a Master of Public Health program. Things were relatively easy at first. It was clear what was expected, and I initially enjoyed the faster pace and increased writing requirements. It wasn't until two years into the three-year program that I began to fall apart.

I knew the stress had been building. Between my failing marriage, worsening finances as student loan debt and credit card bills piled up, the transition of my children from toddlers to school-age, and the military increasing our drill weekends and requirements, it was tough. However, it all crept over me slowly over those first two years of graduate school. It had never occurred to me to slow down the things I could control, like my course load, while the uncontrollable, like my husband's emotional state, my kids aging, and workload came steamrolling over me.

I had my course schedule calculated perfectly to graduate on time. I still needed to take three intense courses I had been avoiding before moving on to my capstone and internship projects. Two involved writing a significant number of papers, and the third was biostatistics—math. I love writing, but I hate math.

Funny, when you're in the thick of it, graduating even six months later than originally planned seems disastrous, but looking back, almost all of this manufactured stress could have been avoided with a little perspective and patience.

The defining moment of my failure came in the form of a breakdown in the Metro State University alumni library. I often went there to study, and I had blocked off a weekend to catch up on all the work I had been avoiding. By then, I had already been granted extensions, offered help by the professor, and admitted to other students that I was stuck. I don't know why I thought just staring at it in a library would help, but I sat there and stared anyway. I stared until I became bleary-eyed, the screen started to blur, my throat began to close, and the heat and tiny stinging pangs of tears started forming around my eyes and falling down my cheeks. The tears—first of sheer frustration—seamlessly flowed into tears of embarrassment that I could not control. So, before too many people noticed, I quickly packed up my laptop and rushed out to my car on that gray, rainy day that perfectly matched my mood to cry by myself to Radiohead.

As the tears subsided and the song concluded, I decided I would not let this affect me anymore. No, not by becoming an optimist or working harder. I just decided to quit. I didn't notify anyone that I had quit; I just stopped showing up. And not just to that class, either. I stopped attending the other two writing intensives that I loved and in which I was doing well, too. I suppose the skewed logic was that if I went in to work on one of the other course assignments, I might see the neon red "F" by all the biostatistics assignments I was avoiding and cry there again.

So instead, I disappeared.

Emails were being sent to the university address I had stopped checking from all three teachers and one concerned friend. For all they knew, I had just dropped dead or disappeared. I spent weeks of blissful ignorance, having pushed the entire thing from my mind. It lasted until the administration emailed my personal account to remind me that the drop deadline had passed and that I would not be refunded for any classes dropped after this date— $900 per class times three courses. I was out $2,700 and only had the destruction of my GPA to show for it. All the sadness I felt that day in the library rushed back and multiplied. I spent the last week of the semester crying, sleeping, and effectively hiding from this expensive, stupid problem I couldn't force myself even to attempt to fix.

The Lesson: Failure Can Force a Break

I overcame this literal failure—Fs all around—by giving myself space and time. I took the next semester off (intentionally) and admitted to myself that I wouldn't graduate before the manufactured air-tight deadline I gave myself at the start of the program. I owned up to the failure and explained honestly and clearly to professors, asking if I could retake their classes eventually. Of course, they all said yes, and those Fs were eventually replaced with As and Bs. I slowed my pace and didn't take all three at once, focusing on one or two at a time while I caught up on the rest of my life.

I graduated two semesters later than I had originally intended, but I graduated. I made it out the other side, and today, school feels so far away, like it was such a short season of my life. Today, the student loans are repaid, and my GPA landed at a low-three-point-something, but literally, no one cares. My degree opened the doors I hoped it would, and not one of my job interviewers asked about that semester.

If you're in the thick of it now, whether still in college, going back to finish your education, or just really feeling the pressure of finals, remember that it only lasts a season, and your job is to push through it in the healthiest way possible for yourself. Stop comparing yourself to others completing it faster or with better grades. Ten years from now, those details won't matter. Take a breath, step back, and give yourself time to feel the stress, cope with it, and just keep going.

Failing at school feels so real and overwhelmingly important when you're in it—while it's happening. Most of us would say it's silly to get upset over grades when there are so many other very real and impactful problems out there to care about, but I remember just how all-consuming that failure felt at the time. It wasn't just about the grades, though. Failing in school felt like admitting to myself that I was a coward who couldn't accomplish something that millions of others succeed at all the time. It hurt.

Now I realize that I didn't have to fail to know I had to pause. If I had been more self-aware or honest with my season of life at that time, I would have known to drop those classes and slow my pace long before I had to pay for those failed course attempts. But, as healing coach, Syanna Wand, so eloquently phrased it,

> *"I've learned to hold regret tenderly:*
>
> *I wish I would have done that differently,*
>
> *and,*
>
> *at the time, I couldn't."*

After that semester concluded, I took time to regroup, skipping another semester before retaking the classes that would get me back on track. Truth be told, facing those huge summits head-on after such a catastrophic failure made the graduation sweeter while adding a callus of knowing that I could get back up and do anything.

Failing stings in so many different ways. It can hurt physically and emotionally, your ego and your relationships. And to truly learn from a failure, you have to take time to really FEEL IT, to let it sink in, but you have to accept the failure first.

As I was failing, I sought out those who were succeeding or had already failed so I could learn from them. So many inspirational types nowadays never hesitate to acknowledge their failures and where they led, but they still aren't as willing to dig into the hurt and devastation of it; they gloss over the humiliation and shameful pieces of the puzzle. They'll tell you to do what you must do to bounce back and that it gets better eventually, and they're right, but no one wants to publicly dig into how much or how long they had to feel it before their resurrection. I don't even want to now as I write these words. Writing this chapter is giving me a pit in my stomach. I've avoided it for so long that now, I'm still handling it in small increments rather than my big writing sit-downs to get it done.

Part of why my failures hurt so hard is because of who I am. I came to terms with being a suicidal person with cyclical waves of depression. I tend to think of my personal climate most closely aligned with Midwestern weather patterns. Some people are in the southwest, where it's almost always sunny and 70 degrees. Sure, you have rainy or windy days, but for the most part, you can count on steady, bright, and happy for your outlook. Others are Alaska. They know they will inevitably face long, cold, dark winters, but they know when to expect it and how to cope. There are lights and plans for facing that darkness, and you know exactly what to expect. In the Midwest, though, the seasons change drastically. And within those seasons, weather comes and goes quickly and harshly. In November, you know winter is coming and that you must brace for it, so you prepare. In my life, this represents the knowledge that something hard is about to happen, and I should take the necessary steps to face it as best I can—but sometimes I don't. I actually don't wear jackets until it hits twenty degrees below zero, so my physical life is syncing up with my mental here.

But the scary weather patterns are the unpredictable tornados. Again, you can see the signs, feel the pressure change, and hear reports and warnings, but you think, "but probably not here," so you don't always plan, prepare, or head to the basement. But even if you think it's not going to be a tornado, there's nothing you can do to stop the clouds, wind, and rain once it's coming in your direction. I can see them coming into my own life. I can feel the sadness in my bones, but I can't do anything about it. The helplessness feeds the fear and sorrow, and soon I just wish for the storm to kill me so I can stop being sad. But then it passes. It always passes. Even when it blows some trees over in its wake, it passes.

I can often guess when it will be better or worse based on times of the day, week, month, or year, but I can never predict the impact of the storm or how bad it will be. The only constants I have to reassure myself are that it will happen again, but it will pass. Only recently have I started gathering supplies and finding places and people to go to when the clouds start swirling. That's all we can do, and I'm doing it. Resistance is the pressure point, not the weather. Hundreds of tornadoes happen in Minnesota every month, but the devastating ones are those where homes and lives got in the way of the wind. The weather is not good evil, it just is, and we get in the way.

To my suicidal readers, to my depressed readers, to my readers hiding in the cellar during the storm—know that it will pass. No storm has ever lasted forever.

If it's a mental climate or environmental issue, you must adapt or move for your own well-being. Before you decide to stop living all life, maybe just stop living this particular life you've chosen. Make those changes that create a completely different person than you are now. Make something better. That idea has given me hope more than once, and I've lived out many versions of myself, but even to do that is to commit to continue failing but doing it in a way in which you set yourself up ahead of time and brace for it beforehand.

We can't run from one storm into another. We must take our time to build strength, get supplies, construct a sturdy house, then go back out with a safe place to return to when we need it.

The Fail: I Was Fired

My first real job (not babysitting or a paper route) was at Byerly's, our local high-end grocery store. At fourteen, I did all the right things to ensure continued employability. I showed up on time, kept my unflattering striped uniform clean, and smiled more than should ever be necessary during a single shift. After only five months, I was promoted from bagger to cashier and felt like this defined me; I would always be the rising star at work, the youngest in my field or my level. Work was easy. I didn't know why grown-ups made it sound so hard.

So, after two years of being an awesome cashier, I was ready to expand my career prospects to the higher—well, higher than $5.75 per hour—paying world of waitressing! I took a job as a hostess at my favorite Perkins restaurant in town.

The host stand was made for the type of
organizational structure on which my brain runs and
thrives. I loved the visual seating chart, the checklist
of who should be sat next, the need for quick
problem-solving when a surprise party of ten came in,
and that the actual customer interaction was just
enough to be mostly smiled at, with little space or
responsibility that would allow me to screw up their
day. It was perfect, and I was great at it. But host
money wasn't server money. I wanted to walk out
with cash like the girls finishing the after-church rush.
So, I asked to be trained and became a cash-making
server within six months, just like I had hoped.

I wasn't terrible at the job from the very start.
My real problem was that I was a hormone-driven,
emotionally volatile sixteen-year-old girl who thought
I was grown. It made me a bad server for many
reasons.

One was because my friends would come to
sit and hang out during my shifts, as wonderful high
school friends do. I comped them food and neglected
my tables while I caught up on who dumped who
during the third hour.

Another was that I fell for my incredibly
attractive and flirtatious 20-something manager, who
had no business flirting back with a 16-year-old girl
in braces. What it meant for me was working to
impress him rather than my customers. Anyone who
has worked in restaurants knows the industry's dating
culture. Everyone is sleeping with everyone else

before, during, or after shifts, then dealing with the fallout of regretful hookups and jealous-turned-vengeful coworkers. I wasn't ready for that level of emotional adult drama, but I sure pretended I was.

Then, the on-again-off-again-love-of-my-life-up-to-that-point ex-boyfriend got a job there because, regrettably, while we were very on, I had made a job referral for him while thinking of how fun and hot it would be to work together and make out in the back office or wink across the serve line. Unfortunately, once we were off, it was torture. He was cute, well-liked, and two years older than me, so of course, the girls without braces who were cuter, more well-liked, and older than me kept us in that "off" area for longer and longer, leaving me crying at my tables and forgetting someone's ranch dressing because I was too busy glaring at the girl who pinched his butt on the way out of the kitchen. Nothing was going well, and my teen world was falling apart.

So, on a sunny slow afternoon, as I screwed up yet another order over my emotional absentmindedness, my manager pulled me into her office. She offered to put me back on as a hostess, so I could have more time to learn, giving me a choice to either finish the week or leave serving immediately. She was about as gracious as you could be in removing someone from a job when they absolutely deserved it. I still spun it in my head as the greatest injustice of human history, stormed out, and cried loudly as I gathered my tips, ripped off my name tag, and sped away immediately.

I called my best friend to vent about the whole thing, but she was busy with her own family (How DARE she?! I wouldn't talk to her for two years after that. Sorry, Lauren!). I distinctly remember thinking I might as well drive off a bridge because I can't do anything right ever, and no one cares about me, anyway. I was suicidal over the nicest rejection of my life at a part-time job when I was sixteen. These feelings were real, though; during that ride home, no one could have convinced me that it would ever get any better.

The Lesson: Sometimes a Failure is Just a Bad Fit

I've been working in suicide prevention for five years now. And whenever I hear someone tell their story of being on the brink of it, or worse, when I read the details of what led up to it for someone who didn't make it to a hopeful ending, I remember how real it felt for me. I recall how I truly and deeply felt like flaking at a serving job unequivocally translated to not being able to do anything successfully in life—ever.

When I was obsessed with reading every book and article on effective parenting, I came across some advice that sounded strange initially but has made more sense since my children have reached their teen years. Essentially, it said you should treat your teen's problems like you would react to an elder facing dementia.

I could relate to this because my senior year employment was in an assisted living facility. I had received all sorts of training on what to do when the residents called me Ruby or told people how long we'd been married. I knew that with dementia (at least in 2003, I'm not up on the developments since then), it was best to allow them to live in their reality, but only until it starts to hurt them.

To clarify, when a kind old man thought I was his long-dead wife, it helped him and eased the situation for me to smile, laugh along, and nod through stories he expected me to remember fondly with him. However, should he grab my waist or become angry that I wasn't reciprocating misdirected marital love aimed at a 17-year-old girl, it had to stop. Usually, in those cases, one of the nurses would intervene and pull him back to reality. We'd tell him where we were and who I was, explaining the situation as gently as possible. Still, the confusion and embarrassment written across his face broke my heart. He didn't mean to make me feel uneasy. It was a brain that wasn't his own and had become lost in time.

Subtract sixty years, and it's not dementia that takes your brain, but an overgrowth of hormones that suffocates that childhood innocence out at its roots or a case of depression that tells you it will never get better—and you believe your lying brain. When you treat your teen like a dementia patient, it implies a certain type of response to their problems. For example, saying, "I know that breaking up with your girlfriend of one month WAS devastating, and it feels like you'll never love anyone else again." As grown-ups, with our post-pubescent brains, we know they'll move on. We all do. However, we must recognize that they are living in an alternate reality where this was the greatest love story of all time—and it just ended.

Let them live it and feel it in all its force, blaring heartbreak ballads, rehashing the entire thirty-day relationship with their friends, crying, screaming, and hiding away from the world. You don't need to do anything to fix it. Let it be, but only until it becomes more serious—until they become obsessive, start to cut their wrists, gain or lose an unhealthy amount of weight or start down the path of substance abuse to numb the pain. You need to pull them back to reality only when coping becomes harmful or goes on for an unhealthy period. At that point, if it gets there, it's time to share the hard truth to bring them back to reality. If they can't do it alone, then it's time for therapy. Failing feels different at all the ages and stages of life, be prepared and know where you fit in your failure journey.

I was that delusional teen, but today, I'm at the top of my field in a career I love. I've had jobs with significantly more responsibility, weight, influence, and consequence behind them, and I've rocked them all. I wasn't meant to be a waitress, clearly. I was meant to write, help, and do plenty of other valuable things in life that would have a more significant impact given my skills.

There's also a birds-eye perspective that is a critical component of realizing which battles to fight. When I was a waitress, I was sixteen with no bills, no one relying on my income, and no real reason to be stressed about losing my job. It wasn't going to impact my world all that seriously. As an adult, I've been furloughed, watched friends receive pink slips, and seen people whose entire lives were supported by a job lose it all in a single day. They would roll their eyes at that dramatic teen.

In the same way that I can look back twenty years and see how silly my sorrow was, I'm sure my retired self will one day laugh at the stress of life in my thirties. Eventually, we all realize that getting fired is literally nothing in the universe's grand scheme of things. And yet, somewhere in between all-encompassing meltdown and nihilistic ambivalence, lies a more moderate viewpoint that understands that those things that impact your life may not impact the world on a grander scale, but they do matter. It's all part of the ride to finding what you are here for.

Finding a good fit means first finding your why. Knowing yourself. Understanding the Ikagi – the Japanese concept of your "life purpose" – of melding things you are good at, things you enjoy, and (for your career) things people will pay you to do. I firmly believe we shouldn't have to settle for just one or two of those options when we choose how to spend our time. Maybe hobbies are the exception, as I do not care if I'm being paid for something I choose to do because it provides joy, contentment, and continuous improvement by doing. Still, the other areas of life should *also* include some level of enjoyment and skill. Our careers should be able to make us money without being the bane of our existence.

And maybe, you've even reached a state of enlightenment to be content to just exist. A flower is on the same Earth as you and it doesn't worry about its offspring or nct worth, it just providcs bcauty and life to the things fortunate enough to encounter it. Maybe you are here just to be, and that's a wonderful thing, too.

K.E. MACPHIE

The Fail: I Was Fired in a Foreign Country

I confess this is my least favorite failure to write about for the simple reason that, quite frankly, I've been lying about it for twenty years.

In the spring of 2003, I worked as an au pair, a fancy title for a foreign nanny, in Wuppertal, Germany. I cared for two little girls, Lotte and Rika, aged three and one, respectively.

I was supposed to live with them for six months, from January through June, but this time was cut short because I was, once again, a completely self-absorbed teenager. As far as practically everyone I know is aware—except maybe my mom and the German family—I was always meant to return home in less than six. For those who were already aware of my plans, I fibbed that I had chosen to come home on my own after four months. So, as far as my personal network was concerned, it was always meant to be a four-month thing, and I loved my time there. I have always conveniently omitted the part where I kindly asked to leave early.

    The great part about this particular chapter is that it occurred during one of the only times in my life when I consistently kept a journal I still have in my possession. To better tell the story, I'll pull some excerpts straight from the pen of seventeen-year-old me to illustrate the saga of the first two months of my life outside the United States. Most of my entries are relatively shallow and revolve around watching MTV, taking the bus into town to use the internet, drinking beer, and missing my friends. It depicted life pre-Facebook, without cell phones, in which the internet was paid for by the minute. Without further ado, here is a carefully curated selection of pen-to-paper quotes to set the scene for my 2003 life in Germany:

February 4, 2003 – Day 10

"I had a slight confrontation with [the dad]. I didn't clean Rika's room, and he says I'm still speaking too much English. I really do have to work on my German more. Granted, it's my first week, but whatever. So, I was a little crabby and angrily cleaned my room."

February 5, 2003 - Day 11

"I got a disposable camera because my friends say they want pictures of me. I also got

batteries and a CD player, so I can finally
listen to Alanis again!"

February 11, 2003 - Day 17

"After dinner, Tabi [my Canadian BFF] called
me. We went out for drinks, although [the
mom] wasn't so happy about it, but we had
another great conversation."

February 12, 2003 - Day 18

"Like a total idiot, I took a nap this afternoon.
I woke up twenty minutes after I was
supposed to take my bus to get the kids.
Charlotte was on a bad day just to piss me off.
She didn't cooperate at all until we got home. I
was pretty sure I was going to scream on a
crowded bus. [The parents] knew about me
being late, and I got a 5-minute lecture. Yeah,
I know, I'm screwing up all the time. I've been
here three weeks. So, after dinner, I just
wanted to be alone. I cleaned, read, and
watched MTV in my tiny room for the rest of
the night."

February 15, 2003 - Day 21

"Once again, I woke up to coffee, Gasoline
[my favorite German band on CD], birds
chirping, and a half-naked, good-looking guy
[my friend, Stefan, who I wrote "looks exactly

like Justin Timberlake!"]. Man, I love mornings."

February 19, 2003 - Day 25

"Those kids definitely have a hold of my mood. After dealing with them for an hour on the way home, I was gonna explode! I realize I don't have to work much, and it's pretty easy work, but my tolerance level isn't built up yet."

February 23, 2003 - Day 29

"Before his bike ride, [the dad] wanted to talk. Yep, third "talk" in a month. He didn't say anything that hurt, I guess, but here I have been trying really hard, and it's not hard enough. I can't help but think this isn't where I belong. I don't fit the job description. I really do like Germany. It's just the stress and all. So, with the whole house to myself, I played sappy songs, read friends' old letters, and just cried until my eyes hurt. I needed it."

February 24, 2003 - Day 30

"OK, I know my mom is my guardian, but if she trusts me enough to send me 3,000 miles away, she should be able to let some stuff go. I can't sleep over - even just at Tabi's - anymore. GAH!"

February 27, 2003 - Day 33

"The best thing that could ever happen... the bar had *The Simpsons* on IN ENGLISH! You have no idea how awesome that was for Tabi and me. I went home in a good mood and told [the parents] all about my night in more German than I've said all month. I think they were happy to see me so happy."

March 15, 2003 - Day 49

"[The dad] asked, "So how do you like it here?" I knew I was done. They had a bunch of examples of why I'm not working out. But the thing is, it's all stuff I could have done but was never told to do! I was kind of just sad because it's like getting fired or something. But honestly, I've been homesick, and I think a semester will be enough. I've learned a lot, and I'm glad I got the experience, so the conversation was bittersweet."

I stopped journaling on Day 52, which is unfortunate because the second half of my stay was so much better. My high school friends and family came to visit over spring break. We toured Amsterdam and Wuppertal together for a week. My German improved dramatically once I actually started speaking it, and I grew to love the family despite my resentment about their heightened cleaning standards and expectations. In early May, I even asked if I could stay on for the originally planned period, and while they agreed I was doing much better, they said the new girl was already planning to come from Ireland.

So, I coasted along at my duties for another month, trained the new girl who had arrived to replace me—and who was quite pleasant—then flew back to Minnesota a few days before the spring semester of my junior year ended.

The Lesson: Maybe You're Just Not Ready... Yet

Overall, I still look back fondly on my time in Germany. As a parent now, I understand the family's frustration with my behavior and level of maturity. Reading the thoughts of a teenager from a 30-something mom's perspective lends a whole different type of truth to the situation. There I was, whining about getting paid to be with the kids for maybe four hours a day, with the opportunity to immerse myself in the environment of an entirely new country and culture. I've lived through my own toddlers and the many toddlers my friends have had over the years, and I fully acknowledge that I was being ridiculous. I would have fired myself, too.

When I was terminated from my au pair position, I was mad. Not only was I pissed at myself for screwing up, but I was angry at them for not understanding how hard it all was for me, and I resented my mom for making me go in the first place.

With this in mind, I've developed a theory I refer to as "Feel It Until." When you fail, the first thoughts tearing at your psyche are the jagged, angry ones, such as jealousy, frustration, disappointment, self-loathing, and anger. You can't really help it. So, to make it through, you just have to keep feeling those feelings and find ways to communicate or process them until it's not so prickly anymore.

You can't stop your first thoughts or your negative feelings overnight. Those are protectors that have been developed over your years of trauma and experience. You can retrain them with a lot of practice, but you shouldn't beat yourself up because you FEEL bad. What you should be cautious about is ACTING bad. Shame and guilt will come if you start saying or doing things in immediate bad feelings than if you just learn to stop and breathe – and cry or scream or find a harmless outlet for the feeling – before you do anything else.

If I could go back to Germany in 2003, I wouldn't try to change the future, but I would offer several bits of advice that came with maturity and experience. I would tell 2003 me that she's being an emotional teenager and that she's allowed to be stressed and upset—but the family must be allowed to live the life they choose in their own home in peace, too. I'd tell her to stop being homesick for the past or dwelling on plans involving what she'll do when she gets home. I'd tell her to be present with the girls, make their days enjoyable, help the family as much as possible, and be a good friend to Tabi and the group. I would recite the classic Andy Bernard line from *The Office*, "I wish there were a way to know you're in the good old days before you've actually left them." You're in them. Enjoy it!

I still have to remind myself of that even after knowing better. 60-something-year-old me with 40-something-year-old kids will remember the "good old days" living with my teenagers full of potential. I will someday miss waking up and seeing them every day, messy rooms and all. Someday, our house, pets, shows, games, and after-school activities will be done and over with—and we'll just remember them as good old days. I recognize that I'm in them, and it's likely you are, too.

Since starting a regular meditation practice, I've been more present in the last six months than in the previous three decades. Previously, I had constantly looked forward, wishing to skip months, seasons, years, and phases at a time. In a sense, I've wasted valuable time wishing to be sixteen to get my license, eighteen to be an adult, and twenty-one to drink legally. I've wished for years of deployment to be over with, for babies to grow up out of diapers, then out of t-ball, then out of car seats. I've wished away semesters of school and the final months of several bad jobs. The crazy part is that all of my wishes came true… but it was never enough. I would fill the resulting void with another wish, looking ahead to the next thing.

A serene happiness is discovered in no longer wishing away years of your life. And there's an odd balance that develops when you can be content with what you have while still working every day to grow and become something more than you were the day before. Of course, I will continue to write about the past while working toward a rewarding future as a professional writer and speaker. Still, if what I have today—with my kids and my pets in this house, writing this book—was to be my every day for the rest of my life, I wouldn't be mad about that, either.

So, while I can't go back to 2003, I can be honest and share those thoughts with my own kids so that they are slightly more present, emotionally mature 17-year-olds someday. Perhaps they'll be less focused on unrequited crushes and MTV (Is MTV even still a thing? Make that YouTube…) and more about the people and experiences laid out in front of them. Maybe they'll fail with more grace than I was capable of back then.

STEP 3: FEEL IT

The Fail: I Had a Meltdown at Target

Yes, you read the title right. No, it wasn't my kid that had a meltdown. It was me—a 20-year-old adult who should have known better. It was my first year as a mom, and it still feels like one of my biggest parenting failures.

In the summer of 2006, we were living in Georgia and had just come home from our big Catholic wedding with hundreds of dollars in cash and Target gift cards. I could finally decorate our base housing exactly how I dreamed it should be, just in time for little six-month-old Colton and his newly discovered in-utero sibling-to-be. My husband was gone for two weeks in the field, and I wanted to surprise him with a beautiful, well-put-together house, so I strapped my baby in his car seat, and we embarked on the 45-minute drive into Savannah for a Target run. It was a hot and sweaty Georgia summer,

86

but I loved the drive through the woods and into the humidity as we drifted toward the ocean.

As we got closer to town, I had already decided this would be a treat myself day. When we landed at my mommy mecca, I purchased a fancy Starbucks drink, planning to casually wander the aisles, not even glancing at price tags. I was flush with gift cards for whatever I wanted! Colton began to get a little fussy, but I had no time for that—I was treating myself! I playfully responded to him at first, laughing and baby-voicing him into silent confusion as I took a few leisurely steps down lampshades and into picture frames. He would calm down momentarily but always come back angrier or sadder than the last time. In retrospect, I inexplicably chose nap time to treat myself, so this was a losing venture from the start.

By the time I was heading to find some cute new maternity gear, his whining was at the point where I didn't respond, closed my eyes, took a breath, and pretended he wasn't mine for two seconds. This response only made him madder and made people look at us judgingly, which mortified me and even made me angry at him—a six-month-old! I knew, under the circumstances, I'd have to cut my day shorter than I had ever dreamed and I was agitated. I was mad at Colton for "purposely" ruining my relaxation, pissed at Target for not having a daycare (but feel free to steal that idea, Target corporate!), and angry at myself for thinking I could ever treat myself.

I was furious I had no one to watch my kid. I was just downright mad and overwhelmed!

I fumed to the checkout, tolerating the ever-increasing volume of his cries while simultaneously pretending they weren't happening. I spoke to the cashier a little louder and forced a smile to pretend I was totally okay with what was transpiring and that I had chosen to ease out of what was meant to be a day of treating myself to head home. She shared the same forced smile and played along with my dumb game. In the end, I spent way more than I intended, but after the gift cards were wiped, I was too embarrassed to start putting things back. Instead, I split the balance between my almost maxed-out credit card and a practically over-drafted debit card. What a treat.

With Colton at full volume by then, the cashier handed me my receipt. We left the store, and I got him strapped tightly into his car seat, which I set on the handlebars of the cart full of all my wonderfully expensive new things. As we teetered out the automatic door, I knew it wasn't entirely safe, but we only had a short way to go. I pushed on carefully, despite his screaming, but miscalculated the lip of the curb that would bring me from the sidewalk to the lot. As it departed the curb at just the wrong angle, my whole cart tipped to the right, dropping all of my brand-new purchases out on the parking lot. Fortunately, the car seat did what it was supposed to and protected my son from hitting the pavement. He was so surprised that he stopped screaming for the first time in what felt like forever, so I took over.

"WHY WON'T SOMEONE JUST FUCKING HELP ME?!?!"

I screamed, and then immediately started hyperventilating in the parking lot as a 50-something woman, and her husband rushed over from where they were about to enter the store. He scrambled to get Colton upright and reload my cart. She put her arm around me and told me to breathe, telling me with a sweet, slight southern drawl, "It's okay. We all have our days. Just calm down, honey." A small crowd had formed to witness my insanity unfolding. My breathing slowed. I wiped my eyes, took a breath, and ungratefully and embarrassingly told them thanks without making eye contact before rushing to my car to push all the things I couldn't afford into my overcrowded trunk. I buckled my still-shocked silent child in while I finished getting the last tears out, then finally drove off.

The Lesson: Be Honest with Where You Are

I am still not sure whether I had undiagnosed postpartum depression or if I was just overwhelmed that, at twenty, I had a newborn baby, a new husband, and a new roommate in an unfamiliar state where I had no friends or family—and absolutely no idea what I was doing. That particular meltdown was the worst outward display of it, but the feeling of, "Why won't someone just fucking help me?" was constant that first year... and I did have help! Even before the six-month mark, my baby had spent three weeks in Washington with his dad's family, we made it back to Minnesota multiple times thanks to free flight benefits, and my husband and roommate were home every night to give me at least a little break.

Now, a dozen years removed from car seats and crying babies, I sometimes forget how incredibly lonely new motherhood can be. Your entire world is consumed by keeping one tiny person alive while they are completely ignorant of all of the dangers that surround them. They sleep wrong, can't feed themselves, and even their own big heads make them very tippy. It's dangerous everywhere! So, take that omnipresent stress and add the expectations for you to make them happy but not spoiled, let them have fun but also learn, and help them to hit developmental milestones at the exact time the baby books say they should... It's a lot, mamas. Trust me, I know.

The good news is... you got this. While one monumental failure changed my perspective on judging parents in Target and opened me up to being more forgiving of bad days, a dozen years of raising those danger babies has taught me just to love and listen to them. Whether you're a helicopter mom, free-range parent, stay-at-home, work all the time, taxi to twenty activities a week or chill at home with nothing scheduled. You can still love and listen—and that's what your kids need.

Loving them means you don't have to like them all the time, and they definitely won't like you— often for days or months at a time during the teen years—but you are there to love them more than anyone else in the world all the time. You are their biggest advocate and cheerleader. Everything you do, from giving them a break to grounding them for a week, should be done out of love. I happen to like my kids, even more so now that they're older, but through every age and stage, I have always loved them the most.

Listening means more than just hearing their words. It's feeling their energy and knowing their limits intuitively. It means you can put down your phone and look at the thing they're making or the run-on story they're telling, but it also means paying attention to what they don't say aloud.

My first son missed a lot of early milestones, but I instinctively knew it wasn't because anything was wrong. He was just a kid who liked to do stuff on his own time and didn't care to compare himself to his peers. He remains that kid to this day as a homeschooled seventeen-year-old on his own schedule and with his own life plans.

My younger son was a baby who hated falling in public view. He learned to crawl, walk, and potty train almost entirely on his own from just observing, but he always preferred to practice when no one was looking. He is still that kid today at fifteen as we teach him to drive and budget and grow into a good human.

As a mom of teens now, I still love them and listen to them every day. I don't like everything they like. In fact, I literally don't think I like ANY of the YouTubers they watch, but I still love them more than anything. And while I will always listen to their input, like why they should be allowed out with their friends until midnight or don't need to clean their room, my decision is always a little different from what they envision—and always final.

The dangers may have shifted from eating solid foods to staying away from drugs and alcohol, but loving and listening are still critical facets of our relationships and always will be. The important part is to give yourself grace wherever you are on the parenting (or living!) spectrum. I was doing what I thought was best at that age, place, and time in my life. Sure, I could look back now and say I was dumb, but the reality is that I was just naive. I was a baby with a baby, and today I know more. The world has changed dramatically just over the course of my lifetime. There have been enormous shifts in how we stay connected and share information, and so many other variables make it impossible to compare me as an older, wiser parent in 2023 to a young mom in 2006.

Whatever you're struggling with today will reveal an obvious solution five years from now. But you're here, not there, so you must learn to give yourself some compassion and accept that you're doing your very best exactly where you are. In the same way we give unconditional love to our kids, give it to yourself. Recognize that you are doing the best you can with what you have, know your limits and how much more you can take on, and then start from here. Don't start from where you think you should be or where your way-more-put-together younger sister is, be honest with yourself, and start your emotional path from where you are with all the love and compassion you can give.

The Fail: I Returned a Foster Dog

I love dogs. I love most dogs more than I love most humans. When I was little, and some creative writing prompt or random adult would ask what I'd do with a million dollars, I had always revealed my big plans to purchase a mansion for dogs, giving them each their own room with a fireplace, patio, and dog bed. Then, I'd sell them for $1 to families who wanted and deserved them. Arguably, it wasn't a great business model, but I was dead serious. I remember carefully sketching out a mansion full of dogs looking out from like 100 windows, complete with a stick figure of me smiling in front.

When I was in my 20s, we left our beloved Pyrenees, Zylo, with a woman who ran a dog boarding business on some significant acreage in the country. Her beautiful little office and the sprawling sunrise views full of dogs became my retirement dream! In typical "like mother, like son" fashion, my kid beat me to it by starting his own pet-sitting business at age eight, and I genuinely loved having those many new friends here all the time until he closed up shop when he turned fourteen and moved on to his next career.

When the opportunity came to foster dogs in need living in high-kill shelters, I knew I could do it. I wanted to do it. I held so much judgment against the people who put their pets there or, worse, abandoned them to find their own way into a shelter. I had a great deal of high and mighty feelings about rectifying what they did wrong to their innocent pets. I guess the universe decided I needed to get kicked down a couple of pegs.

I started by fostering kittens. We kept a litter of five farm kittens I saw needed care and bottle feeding on Facebook. Their names were Chestnut, Acorn, Walnut, Cashew, and Pecan. In preparation for the endeavor, I cleaned out the dining room of our house, drove a half hour away to pick them up with all their gear, and committed to administering daily medications and attending weekly PetSmart adoption day hangouts with all of them.

I knew the phrase "it's like herding cats" from my time as a t-ball coach, but I finally gained a solid understanding of where it came from. It was no small job. We had them for ten adorable days, where I took every opportunity to invite friends over to sit with them, play with them, post videos and bios of each little personality, and enjoy temporarily loving some mischievous baby cats. The hard work was worth all the cuteness, and it was easier than I expected to find deserving, joyful families when the time came. We could definitely do more, I remember thinking.

So, we moved into the dog fostering realm. Shadow was our first. He was a docile and smiley black and white Shepherd mutt with a forever home interview pending. Shadow was an easy guest. His only odd habit was perching on top of the couch to look out the picture window, but it was quirky, cute, and harmless. I had nothing but good things to say and funny stories about him when I brought him to his new home. As he got to know his prospective family, an empty nest couple with one other lonely, young dog, everything was perfect. He loved them. Their dog was curious and then ecstatic to have a friend, their house was gorgeous, and Shadow was so excited about the massive backyard. By the end of the paperwork, the new family was crying. I was crying. Shadow was happy. It was just how I dreamed foster life would always be.

Then we got Steve.

I met Steve in the high-kill county shelter in Minneapolis. I had never been there and thought I was ready to see the cold concrete warehouse where they keep the kennels. It ripped my heart out that as we walked past every dog—mostly pit bulls like Steve—they would either run to the gate in the desperate hope that you were here for them, or they'd cower back farther in the corner because they had learned that people meant pain and they were still working through it. Smiley Steve was one of the happy ones. He was thrilled to be out of his kennel, grateful for every kind touch and moment of attention, and so energetic in the small workout space they provided. When the foster agency asked on the spot if I would be willing to take him, how could I say no?

I knew his energy was a lot more than what we're used to, but in our pet-sitting experience, energy lasted a few hours, maybe the first day or two, then they learned the routine, settled in, and found their calm. Steve never did. From day one to sixteen, he chewed everything he could get his mouth on, sprinted through our tiny rambler, and knocked over any furniture or humans in his way. He cried whenever he was in his kennel, hated going outside alone, and forced someone to stand in the cold with him. The kids helped when they could, but they were tired, too. He was a lot of work.

Two weeks after we got him, still at 100% energy, we went out of town. I posted on Facebook, asking if any of my friends would be able to watch him, especially looking for families that might be interested in adopting. Two of them graciously volunteered to help, and I was optimistic that either he'd be a great fit with one of them or at least the break would give me the energy to come back with a renewed love for him and his antics. The families were as exhausted as I was after only a week each, and the break for me wasn't nearly long enough.

Within a week of returning from our travels, I hated being in my own home. I cried when he wouldn't stop acting out based on his mood at the time, whether it was energetic, sad, needy, or whatever. I was tired. He wasn't getting adoption hits, visits, or inquiries. When I took him to adoption days at PetSmart, he scared people with his aggressive love and desperation. I didn't know how I could take it much longer. I emailed the foster dog coordinator and said I couldn't do it anymore, and they responded that they could maybe get a trainer after six weeks. I knew I had agreed to this. I didn't have to say yes at the shelter... it was my fault, I didn't deserve the help, the weight was getting heavier.

So, we kept trying. We got Steve a special rawhide treat for Christmas, and he loved it. Too much. It gave him something to do and occupied his time. He'd bring it back to his kennel and gnaw for 20-minute blocks of time. Great! It wasn't until I went to let him out, and as I got close, he growled at me. That was a first. I noticed he was getting defensive of the rawhide to the point that it became a little scary, but I could usually wait for him to get bored and sneak it out while he was preoccupied with something else.

Then one day in January, as he was in his kennel with the rawhide, my son reached over to let him out for the afternoon. Before he unlatched the door, Steve aggressively barked and bit at him through the bars, but it was enough to break the skin. I had a hard line about dogs biting my kids, so I had hit my breaking point. I called the foster group and said he needed to go now. I would bring him back to the kill shelter if they did not pick him up. They were clearly upset with me, but I didn't care anymore. Within 24 hours, they arranged for someone "more experienced" to take him. I was banned from being a foster again, and I spent the next month sleeping, crying, and feeling like a complete failure and an awful human being for giving up on Steve.

The Lesson: Go to Therapy

In retrospect, I had agreed to take Steve at a low point of my cyclic depression. You know how when you're sad, rather than sit around and feel it, you try to think of ways to make yourself happy? Puppies make me happy, so it seemed to follow that becoming a foster would fix the sadness! Winters aren't great in general for my mental health. During that particular season, I had been hit by an avalanche of financial issues coming to a head, dealing with a recent crushing breakup, and choosing to withdraw from running for office.

The thing is, if I told the foster group, "Hey, I just got this dog, but now I have cancer. Can you re-home it?" I think they would have jumped through hoops to help. When it was triggered by depression, not only did I keep it to myself, but I didn't feel confident that people would scramble to help me heal like they would with a more tangible illness. At least, that's the story I told myself, which led to how I responded to my own experiences with mental illness. Depression still sounds like a cop-out to many—but that's a stigma I want to break.

Mental health issues need to receive more out loud acknowledgment, attention, and awareness. I want friends to start social media campaigns to help get each other better, for people to post selfies and invite friends to scary therapy sessions like we show up for each other at chemo clinics. I would love to see 5Ks, where they give suicide survivors bright-colored shirts and surround them with those who gave their money and time to loudly proclaim they want to help. Make depression like cancer. If we put it in the spotlight, maybe we'll come as far in suicide, mental illness prevention, and early intervention in the next twenty years as the color pink has done for breast cancer in the twenty prior.

That's not all, though. I also want to teach people that it is perfectly acceptable to just sit in your sadness and feel it, to let it overcome you without destroying you. We don't need to fix it immediately when it takes hold. Nor do we need to numb it with food, alcohol, drugs, cigarettes, or agreeing to foster dogs. We need to breathe through it. Cry it out. Talk to people about the raw emotions and really dig into what's happening, even as we flounder in the middle of the sadness. The catch is you must learn to acknowledge the pain without going too far into sadness and risking deep depression or, worse, suicidal ideation or attempts.

I've learned much more about this through my experience with EMDR (Eye Movement Desensitization and Reprocessing). When treated with EMDR therapy, the patient returns to a painful time in their mind. Then, while their neurons feel like they're there experiencing those emotions and feelings, they can process the event in a healthier way. I highly recommend the book *The Body Keeps Score* by Dr. Bessel van der Kolk for a deep dive into EMDR, but I can tell you a little of my personal experience, too.

While the purpose of EMDR is to reprocess traumatic events, in my therapy leading up to my first trauma session, we practiced going back for a positive experience to get those brain processes working. Recalling it today, the session feels like a true memory in my mind, not just a dream or imagined event. I feel like I – at 37 – spent the day with a kid who needed me. And I feel like I – at 4 – had an amazing day with an adult who cared about me and gave me all of her attention and validation for a day.

In a healing session, I went back to a traumatic day when I was eight and was berated and embarrassed by an adult. It was a time I felt shame and frustration that translated to a life of not trusting myself; of always being afraid that I'm not as smart or as brave as I first thought I was. As I relived the memory, my therapist asked my current self to intervene. And like the amazing day with a smaller me, I stood up for the eight-year-old to be the adult she needed then. I told her she was brave and smart, that she did the right thing, and it's ok that not everyone can understand that. I made her a sandwich, I gave her a hug, I healed that deep emotional wound.

By the end of the session, we healed each other, me healing me, to the point that it's filled a void that's lived inside me for years. Soon after that session, I quit smoking because the healing filled the small constant desire to die; I quit drinking because my newfound peace has become a place I'm not trying to escape with substances. And I'm not the only one with such dramatic results with EMDR. The key is taking the first step into it to trust the process, and then to keep going through the hard and the dark stuff to get to the healing.

While I recommend therapy to everyone I meet, I also think you can reprocess hard events through a commitment to meditation and mindfulness. We don't need a clinician to offer us self-compassion or to reframe an experience from one that generates feelings of guilt or ineptitude to one in which we did the best we could with what we had to offer at the time, but they sure help give credibility to the little voice in you that knows how great you really are.

The Fail: I Divorced My Husband of Ten Years

Content disclaimer on this story: This book is about MY fails, not my ex-husband's. He did plenty wrong in our marriage, and he has heard it all from me before, so I hope you can read this chapter with grace for me as an imperfect narrator telling one side of the story. And if you are in a divorce or a breakup for a fallout with a friend that still feels painful and raw, I hope you can aspire to one day forgive them enough to not write them as the villain in your story, either.

When we married, I remember thinking: *I love him so much. I will never want to live without him.*

We were both products of divorce, but we were convinced that our parents and other divorced couples truly didn't love each other as much as we did. Everyone else wasn't us. We were different, and I couldn't fathom that we could ever feel otherwise. We weren't just another statistic.

I filed for that unfathomable divorce on January 3, 2015.

We met at military training at Ft. Sam Houston, Texas, in 2004. I was his training squad leader, and he was my problematic, talkative, but sweet soldier. Our friendship naturally progressed to flirtation, eventually leading to me crying on graduation day when he said we'd never see each other again.

We kept in touch, and I saw him a month later in Georgia, where he had been sent for training. Then, I saw him again on leave in Washington and met his family. I kept flying to see him until April 29, 2005, when we eloped at Ft. Stewart, Georgia, where he was stationed for active duty. We were always holding hands, laughing, cuddling, kissing, and being more obnoxious than we intended as far as the rest of the world was probably concerned. Once, on a Greyhound bus ride to Atlanta, the last time I would see him before his first deployment, an older man in the seat behind us told us, "Be careful, or you'll run all out of kisses." We laughed, believing that could never happen to us. It became a cute inside joke for many years.

We had the kind of love that lasted through two deployments, two babies, a new house, and a cross-country move. I wouldn't grow to resent him deeply for a few years.

The first deployment was easy. It only lasted a few months and was located in a low-conflict zone. I was pregnant at home and had plenty to stay busy with between work, school, and my adorable brownstone in Uptown Minneapolis. He left and came back just in time for me to have our first baby. Everything was perfect.

During the second one, we started strong. I sent boxes of cookies, new-release Xbox games, mushy letters, and photos of the kids. It all seemed fine until one distinct phone call, where he didn't sound like himself. His friends had been hit by a roadside bomb and were being treated at a different hospital—and no one knew their status. A stop-loss order had just come down as they were part of "the surge" of 2007. They knew they would all be there longer than the one year they were promised. Everyone was upset but not screaming or crying, just feeling half dead. I could hear that my sweet, funny, happy husband was gone. I only hoped he could find that man again before he came back.

A few months later, when he came home and left the Army in 2008, I thought I got him back, so I created unrealistic expectations of what he would do. I expected him to love staying home with the kids, but he barely knew them. I expected him to get a great war hero-type job, but he wanted to rest. I expected him to fix and maintain the house and mow the lawn, but he had never done any of those things before. So, my silent expectations—the ones I never told him about because I thought he should just know to do them—grew into resentment and disdain against him for merely being who he always was.

Resentment is poison in relationships. As I became more disappointed in him, he grew frustrated with me. As I got quieter and more complacent around him, he called me cold and distant, among many other names and criticisms. His anger was closer to the surface than it had been before. His humor was darker and more twisted. My husband didn't come home. Some sad, angry Veteran returned in his place. Soon, we only liked each other when we drank, but some of our biggest fights erupted after we had over-imbibed. We spiraled for years into a cycle of disgust, jealousy, secrecy, and painfully apathetic attitudes that only gave us fuel to use against the other.

When I was in love with my husband during the first five years, I thought, I don't even remember what it's like to have crushes on other guys. I had been so infatuated for so long that I had no feelings beyond a brief acknowledgment of their symmetrical features when I saw an attractive person. During the final years, all I saw were better options. Guys who were better dads, husbands, and soldiers. Men who were in better shape, funnier, smarter, and cooler than my husband. All I did was compare, so I spent more time finding glimmers of greatness in other guys than in my own. In year nine, after I had already brought "the D-word" into a fight and, therefore, into the realm of possibilities, my high school ex-boyfriend found me on Facebook and asked for "help" since he had just got out of the Navy and heard I worked for the VA. I was more than happy to find the best in him.

We flirted online without *really* flirting for months, relying on old inside jokes, "remember when" conversations and random compliments to make each other smile. It all amounted to enough that I got butterflies when I saw his name on my screen, but not so much that I considered what I was doing cheating. Eventually, he said it would be easier to discuss the options in person. I said we could meet for lunch near where I worked. When I saw him, all the fireworks came back in full force. It felt like electricity, and I knew he felt the same. I couldn't stop smiling and felt a powerful magnetism that made it seem like I could only feel good when I was close to him. When we hugged goodbye, I had butterflies for the rest of the day. I remembered all those feelings that came along with wanting someone and being wanted that I hadn't felt in so long, and the fact of the matter was that all I wanted was to have them again. That meeting flipped a switch in me, causing me to actively choose to find ways out of my drowning marriage rather than finding reasons to stay and fight for air.

When terrified married people ask me when I knew it was the right time to file, I tell them, for me, it was when I found myself wishing he had died. If he had died in Iraq, he would have died a hero, a wonderful husband, a dad his kids would hear about for the rest of their lives as the bravest man anyone knew. Instead, he lived to become the villain. He was angry and coping with drugs and alcohol. He had burned bridges with most of his friends as he didn't want any connection to the military. My husband came home, but the man I married never came back.

I started loudly telling people all the bad stuff from our marriage—all the negatives that I had kept hidden for a while. The stories of our fights and disdain were all told from my side. No one was defending him, especially not himself. It was all selectively true, but it dramatically changed the lens my friends saw us through. They had all witnessed his ugly side at some point, which only validated my perspective. By the end of the year, everyone was telling me to get a divorce. I reluctantly agreed and bravely filed.

I would spend the next four months going on dates again and feeling butterflies with the Navy ex and others, dreaming of a life away from this awful husband who kept begging me to stay. I called him obsessed and smothering. I told him we were toxic to each other. When he promised to improve, I told him to be better for someone else. I was beyond done.

I cried all morning on our divorce day, April 1, 2015. I left work because I couldn't stop crying. I listened to Radiohead and cried in my car. I cried at the courthouse. He was so sad, too. He cried in the morning, begging me not to do it, then didn't even show up. I showed up—and I cried more. None of those new guys or the butterflies were there to console me, just my lawyer, who reminded me of the remainder due on my payment plan before leaving for her next case.

I left the courthouse legally single and never feeling more alone.

K.E. MACPHIE

The Lesson: Feel It with Some Self-Compassion

I'm not advocating that you run out and aim to fail in everything. I didn't get married with the intent to get divorced. Your failures could be long, drawn-out fights or they can be just slight bumps in the road. They don't have to be all-out collapses but know that you will fail and accept that it's okay. If you only traveled down a perfect path, you would never have the opportunity to get creative or brainstorm bigger, better options—and you'd never know just how sweet it can be when you finally succeed. When you build in failing as part of your path, you won't be so shocked when it inevitably shows up. Everyone will fail at some point, but those who are prepared will fail better!

I did not let myself feel my divorce for a long time. I'd say most divorced friends don't give themselves time to really process it, likely because it's a horrible, gut-wrenching ache that needs more attention than we have capacity. None of us like to feel those deepest emotions that tighten in our throat or put a rock in our stomach, but they are especially tricky when they conflict with what we're supposed to feel. You're supposed to be sad at a funeral, so it's okay and expected that people would cry. No one is surprised, and everyone knows why without asking. But here, I'm the one who filed for divorce. If I was so sad over the situation, why didn't I just stay? Why wasn't I having an epic dress-burning divorce party, which had just become a fad on Pinterest? He was so awful at the end. How could I possibly miss him?

No one actually asked me those questions, but I thought they would. The story I told myself was that I had no right to cry; even if I did, I had no desire to dig into the reason behind it. Maybe I knew in my heart that the person I missed had left long ago when he boarded that last flight to Iraq. Or it's possible I wasn't happy because even if, in the end, I was done, there was a long time in the beginning and middle where I dreamed of forever—and while that dream had slowly eroded with his drinking and PTSD, a stamp from the courts is what finally killed it.

Instead of allowing myself to feel sad or talk through the situation, I started dating new guys. The butterfly feeling that accompanied newness and attention was a great cure for heartbreak until it wasn't. I started drinking a lot more because, at first, drinking made me giggly and funny. In the end, it only made me feel sad and alone. I smoked a lot, partly because the guys I was dating did and also because it goes so well with overdrinking. I ate my feelings into 250 lbs. of "treating myself" and buying whatever groceries I wanted now that I didn't have to ask my husband what he wanted for dinner. The year after my divorce was defined by fucking, drinking, smoking, eating. All things I thought meant freedom when I was doing them, but looking back, I can see they were more of a cage to contain all the pain I didn't want to feel.

Then, my ex was in a bad car accident two years after our divorce. He was fucking, smoking, and drinking his way through pain, too, until he hit his own rock bottom and used it as the foundation to learn better coping skills like talk therapy and meditation. I could see the difference and the newfound peace within him. I wanted that peace as well, so I started my own rehabilitation.

That year, I wasn't in a crash, but I ended things with my two on/off hookups to give back the time I had been spending at their apartments to my kids. I slowed down the girls' nights out, replacing them with yoga and quiet meditation in my room. During that time, I admitted to myself that I needed to process the end of my marriage. But, as all healing isn't linear, I was improving up until my run for office, that load-bearing failure detailed in chapter 1, and I crashed back to earth along with all my progress.

December was hard. I went to four Christmas parties sober, saw smoker friends for the first time, and had to decline hanging outside with them. I was just starting to feel all the emotions and sit with them rather than drink through them, which made me a little crazy. I was suicidal and depressed, so I searched for a healthier coping mechanism to replace them.

January was even worse. I desperately wanted to get better but couldn't pick myself up. I was fully aware of how awful I felt and yet seemed unable to fix it. Everyone else was starting over and celebrating their clean slate with the coming of the new year. I was hiding, believing that treading water to stay afloat and not killing myself was the best I could ever expect to be.

On one of my worst days, I remember watching musicals to force myself to feel better. I used to do the same thing with my mom and sisters as a kid, and we'd sing goofy songs and make inside jokes over the dramatic dancing and wonderful, memorable lyrics.

So, there I was on a Sunday, hadn't showered or gone anywhere for three days, when I thought a new musical would perk me up and get me out of bed. I Amazon Primed the movie *Hello Dolly* starring Barbara Streisand. It featured all of the typical musical joy, and when it got to an upbeat song, I listened to the lyrics:

"Put on your Sunday clothes when you feel down and out.

Strut down the street and have your picture took.

Dressed like a dream, your spirits seem to turn about.

That Sunday shine is a certain sign that you feel as fine as you look!"

And I started sobbing. I wanted that Sunday feeling but didn't even have clean clothes. I hadn't done laundry in over a week! I desperately wanted to be happy enough to dance my way out of Yonkers (… you really do have to see the movie), but the best I could do was hug my cat and cry in bed.

This is that unexplainable paralysis of depression. A motivational speaker version of myself would have cheered, "You got this! Will power! Just do it! Get up and put your Sunday clothes on!" The depressed version could only see a pit of despair where I'd never have clean clothes again because it felt so daunting. The ME that I needed was self-compassion. One who said to that girl crying in bed, You're doing your best. You are not in a musical. You won't feel like this forever. Let's cry for another minute, then brainstorm another path forward that doesn't involve doing laundry right this minute.

February got better. I rediscovered reading, writing, yoga, and meditation – the other paths forward. I started reading self-help books in a desperate search for someone to empathize with or explain what I was going through. I picked up *Your Best Year Ever* by Michael Hyatt because I thought, as implausible as this sounds, maybe I should start over today. Michael's book was exactly what I needed. He offered ten areas in which people could focus on improving their lives based on the eight dimensions of wellness I mentioned earlier (the other two are parental and marital wellness). Then, he provided statements of how you should feel at peak performance in those areas, stating them in the present tense—not as if it was a goal, but like you were already there.

"I am happy more often than I am not."

"I enjoy my kids and know being a parent is my greatest work."

"I have a best friend who I can call about anything."

He made goals feel real, pulling me out of a deep pit where I had lost sight of any possibility of achieving true happiness. His book was the first light I saw at the end of a long, dark tunnel, and for once, I wasn't hoping the light was a freight train coming full speed for me.

I made it through the worst of my feelings. Allowing myself to feel things without the crutch of my prior unhealthy coping methods was downright awful. There's no other way to put it, but it's the only way out. The withdrawals of dealing with reality are at a soul-crushing level of pain. You can pretty much expect to feel like wishing you could rip yourself out of your own skin, then resign yourself to the fact that you cannot, and be forced to live with that until it begins to fade. And they will.

That's it. You HAVE to let yourself feel it. All of it. And you have to know that it's not going to be easy, it isn't going to be linear, but it's also not going to go on forever, either. Some days will be better, others worse, but in the long run, it will improve. Feel it all. You got this.

K.E. MACPHIE

STEP 4: FIX IT

K.E. MACPHIE

The Fail: I Was Cut from the Volleyball Team

I was never meant to play volleyball, but that didn't mean I had to be a bitch about it.

I began my illustrious career on the private school junior high team, where everyone who showed up got to play. We competed against the same three other private schools over and over, and I don't remember anything except that we had cool cheers, and the uniforms were cute. Somehow, that was enough to make me sign up for the freshman team in my first year at Kennedy.

Joining volleyball sounded like a good way to make friends, especially since practices would begin in August before school started. I would have an opportunity to meet a group of moderately athletic girls who didn't know each other yet, and we would be forced to become friends, at least on some level. Friendship by force was my favorite kind of friendship. Some of those girls are still my best friends to this day, but those early friendships developing would be the high point of my time in the sport.

Freshman year, fourteen and nerdy, transitioning from private school to public, I was still deciding what my new public-school persona should be. Somehow, despite not having cable and being generally happy, I landed on Daria, the dark, sarcastic MTV teen. It wasn't me, but "the real me" was a dork. I had to be whatever the opposite of that was, so I committed myself to feign apathy and to exude a very "like, ya know, whatever" attitude. Apparently, coaches hate this vibe (primary source: I have since coached many other apathetic wannabes much like my-then-self).

On the occasions that I did put forth a significant effort, I acted rude or frustrated in the most dramatic of ways, to the point that it once got me pulled from a game. I served the ball, and it hit the net (because practicing was for nerds), so I yelled and slammed my hands on the ground like a stubborn ape. Jen, the pretty 20-something coach who lived and breathed volleyball, was already halfway sick of my shit based solely on my chronic back-talking and feigned asthma during laps, so she pulled me rather than reprimand me again. I'd spend the rest of the season spreading the rumor that she was sleeping with the varsity coach and calling her an uptight bitch behind her back. I was truly awful.

I finished the season a little better than how I started, with a handful of friends but a bunch of coaches who thought I was a snotty teen they were glad to be done with. Fast forward to sophomore year. It was B-squad tryouts, and all my friends were back in August to go out for the team. Between the end of the freshman season and the final days of the summer before 10th grade, I dated two older guys and lost my virginity to one of them. I acquired a real job and picked up smoking. I had a driver's permit and a reputation. My attitude was not any better, but in fact, worse because it had some real anger and sadness behind it. I was no longer merely filling in the blanks based on "what would Daria do?" But I wanted to hang out with my friends to rehash the drama of the previous summer, so I eye-rolled and whined my way from missing serves to coming in last during sprints all through tryouts. Somehow, I was still shocked that my name wasn't on any rosters and was cut from the team.

To be fair, I was primarily surprised because they only cut two people: a girl who signed up but didn't come to tryouts and me. It was a very intentional "fuck you" from the coaches, who I'm certain had no desire to put up with me for another season. Before anyone could look beyond their own name, I left the gym with angry tears pouring out while biking to work. I told people I had quit the stupid league and didn't want to play for that uptight bitch, anyway.

The Lesson: Fix Your Attitude

As my kids are in their teenage years, I'm trying so hard to channel who I was back then and remember—or dissect—why I was so awful. Because truly, I was the absolute worst for a while there.

I've realized that every time I did something bad when I knew better, it was because I felt lost. It was like we were all in a play, but someone forgot to give me the script, so I was mad at everyone else because I was the only one who looked stupid up on stage. I just kept hoping I'd fall into what I was supposed to be doing, the thing where everything came easy, and I was the best person in the room— whether it was volleyball, choir, softball, a class, or something else entirely… anything! But, for everything I tried, there was always someone better, a natural, more talented, or experienced, and as soon as it got hard or I wasn't "as good as" someone else, I

126

told myself it clearly wasn't the "thing" for me, sabotaged it, and kept looking.

Unfortunately, in my search for "the thing," what actually got the attention of the whole room was being a braces-wearing round-faced kid smoking a cigarette; being the first, and for a long time only, one from my friend group, who was having sex; taking my car out at fifteen while Mom was at her second job and cruising past my friends on bikes to show off; cutting my wrists and poorly hiding them with Hot Topic bracelets and thumb sleeves. For a while, I was the best at being shocking, and it fed that need to be the best a lot easier than trying to figure out the things no one was telling me to do on my own.

Now, as a parent to teens, I am cognizant of telling my children that they are seen, are exactly where they need to be, and are doing exactly what they should be doing. Even screwing up, failing, and getting in trouble is what they should be doing as they grow and learn. And if they feel lost or behind everyone else, they need to know that we all feel that way sometimes and that comparison is a thief of joy. Together, we are learning to be grateful for what we have, happy with where we are, and content with whatever comes next.

Sometimes, fixing things means fixing your attitude. And before you roll your eyes like I would have done to myself, know that fixing your attitude won't fix everything. And know that by attitude, I don't just mean a sassy teenager—sometimes your attitude is just negative self-talk.

The attitude I most recently had to address was the "hot mess mom" vibe that came to be adorkable and trendy in millennial parenting. Rather than make an effort to be on time or get off Facebook and bake some cookies for the fundraiser, I leaned on this quirky, cute persona that allowed me to own being a hot mess. If I'm being honest, I didn't have to be a hot mess, but it was easier than being a "try-hard" (as my kid calls it) and social media along w movies like *Bad Moms* made it look cool. Everything I thought was funny pitted the perfect pearl-wearing PTO moms against us hot mess moms, so if I had to pick a camp, I picked the one that got sloppy drunk at happy hour. However, once I stepped back, I realized I was embracing the hot mess mom persona for other people and definitely not for my kids. They didn't think it was cute when I'd stop for drinks before their show or forget to pick them up from practice because I was on a date. But it made for a funny Facebook post with a lot of likes, so I kept doing it.

Fixing your attitude means digging back to the bigger purpose of who you want to be and why. Giving up the hot mess vibe meant taking the time to quit trying to find the shock value, and instead, doing something I didn't love for the benefit of my kids. Once I looked up and stopped making it into an us vs. them mom fight, I found some wonderful pearl-wearing women. They were generous and kind, had awesome advice for handling new parenting hurdles, and were welcoming and happy to get to know me. That's when I realized I wasn't as hot a mess as I tried to make myself out to be. I actually had a lot going for me and was doing pretty well in life. My sweater-wearing former foes offered valuable perspectives and genuine interest. They were overwhelmingly impressed by how much I had accomplished without many of the benefits they had as moms.

And I realized that they weren't as perfect as I villainized them to be. One, whom I had been so jealous of for her tiny figure, later told me she was overcoming an eating disorder. How heavy is that to carry around while still being silently hated for being "perfect?" And even the ones that do have it together behind the scenes overcame some stuff to get there. Most of them leaned heavily on their faith or family, others had strong silent partners helping them. And like with my teenager analogy, just because their problems seemed lighter to me doesn't mean they weren't real to them. Maybe they didn't live the single mom paycheck-to-paycheck life, but it's a different kind of pain to watch your retirement fund drop by the thousands due to no wrong action on your part. We're all in it, and shifting my attitude reminded me that we're in it together, not in separate pools.

At the same time, I saw my hot mess crew wasn't as messy as I'd been, either. It was actually my younger son who questioned us. He knew we called ourselves the Hot Mess Moms and, knowing the other women of the group, he told me we're all good moms. He said, "maybe you're like, a medium mess, but all of you go to our games and volunteer at stuff, so you're not actually that bad." And he was right. Some of my messy mom friends were sober. Most of us met through volunteer work. All of us were involved with our kids' lives and doing our best. We weren't wearing pearls, but the moms I grouped in with my messiness were actually some of my biggest role models, I just had to shift my view from this sitcom-trope of what I thought we were and look at them for the complex people they, and I, really are.

Fixing your attitude is most easily accomplished by consciously shifting to a space of gratitude and calm. I started learning this through meditation, but I tried to go in 100% with gurus like Eckhart Tolle and Dali Lama but got frustrated because it felt like reading dissertations while I was at a grade school reading level. So, I found my route to meditation through the app, Headspace. I can offer some small baby steps to move toward their enlightenment levels, because now (a few grades higher) I love reading Tolle and the more advanced theories and practices meditation has to offer.

One way to ease in is to start challenging yourself to find small gratitude, like in those frustrating day-to-day moments. The most common for me is when someone cuts me off in traffic. I used to get so mad at those inconsiderate pricks, but now I say this aloud in the car for my kids to hear: "Wow, I'm glad I'm not in such a rush that I need to drive in traffic like that." Gratitude.

Another common one is having low patience with your kids. When one—or more—are being real jerks, not listening, and going against everything you say, stop and think, "Wow, I'm so lucky to have such strong, independent children who can assert themselves." Sometimes, I even tell them that and then take the time to explain why, in spite of it, they need to get over themselves and do what I said in the first place.

The key to gratitude is to make it genuine. I'm not saying those things with sarcasm and condescension, but honestly, because the thoughts are only with myself. Sometimes my instinctual thought is really "wow, what an asshole" but my first deliberate thought that I want to put energy out to the world, is the micro gratitude.

And here's the other thing about the fix: it has to be in direct proportion to the pain. Let's think of it as a physical example, as I learned from my wonderful TikTok therapist, Matthias. When you fall off your bike as a kid, you scrape your knee. You cry for a few minutes, mom puts on some Neosporin and a Band-Aid, and you go back to kid business. It feels like a big hurt in your little life, but the fix is fairly easy.

Fast forward twenty years, and you skid your motorcycle on the freeway. That scrape of childhood has now become a massive road rash across huge sections of your body. Mom can't help you, but maybe a good medical team at your nearest ER can.

Neosporin is replaced by some schedule II narcotics. A Band-Aid won't fix it. In fact, it could require skin grafts, full body traction, and months of follow-up appointments. The failure of falling off your bike feels somewhat familiar, but the fix is drastically different. The key is not pretending a band aid will fix your road rash, and also knowing you shouldn't ask for a full body cast when you only skinned your knee. Be real and honest about how much fix you need to put into your emotional wounds.

Getting cut from sophomore year volleyball felt like a massive failure at the time, but with some perspective, I can see it was a kid-level injury. The divorce, election loss, debt and so many adult problems are the real road rash. Sometimes, it's important to consider that perspective in the big picture. Take a step back because the hurt will always sting worse when you're directly in it but try to gauge how drastic of a fix you need. I needed an attitude adjustment back then. As an adult, I've needed professional help from finance counselors, therapists, and others who could take the time to put me in traction when I needed it most.

Meanwhile, under-fixing doesn't help either. Too many friends go through a massively traumatic failure like a divorce or bankruptcy and move on quickly back to their regularly scheduled programming—their real, regular life. Take time to heal from those events, there is no time limit and no race to heal.

Take however long it takes to understand, to seek the right fix, and to do the work to truly heal.

The Fail: I Was Morbidly Obese

Some people will read this chapter and think, "You only weighed 250? Skinny bitch...," while others might say, "WHOA, 250! That's like two Kardashians!" It isn't all about the number, though. It's about the feelings behind it and the hundred pounds before it as a consistently dense 5 foot 4. I wanted to offer certain insights to those who have never been close to morbid obesity and perhaps some relatability to others who have been at my weight and beyond.

Even at, and getting up to, 250, I've been happy, outgoing, dated great good-looking guys, wore cute clothes, and went on fun vacations. And even at 150, I've been self-conscious and miserable. The number isn't the mindset—and the mindset is everything.

My current homeostasis is to carry myself with the confidence of a skinny girl but enjoy the public anonymity of a fat one. I don't have any medical issues because of the weight, and my only self-imposed limitations have always been to fit on rollercoasters and never require a seat belt extender on airplanes (so far, so good).

My size isn't considered a failure because I got bigger, but rather because I've let weight define my life for far too long and honestly, it's an ongoing failure that I'm still working to fix.

** CONTENT DISCLAIMER: This section may be triggering for those struggling with eating disorders as I will detail my exact weight and eating habits or unhealthy exercise choices of the past. If that is a concern of yours, please skip to "The Lesson: Fix Your Why" **

Growing up, I always felt like the fat friend next to my thinner, smarter, prettier private school friends. Looking back at pictures, I'm pretty sure I just had chubby cheeks and a tendency for petite pals. I have always been heavy but not always fat, but I wasn't even aware of the scale number until entering the military.

Age 17, 150 lbs.

Enlisting in the Army in 2003 was supposed to be easy. At the time, they were desperate for soldiers to fight in the new Iraq war. My

ASVAB (Armed Forces Vocational Aptitude Battery aka the test that would determine what jobs you were offered) were solid enough to warrant any career path I wanted. I didn't do drugs or have a criminal record, my eyesight was perfect, I wasn't colorblind, but then I failed the height/weight portion of the physical. I wound up leaving MEPS (the Military Entrance Processing Station) empty-handed but with an opportunity to come back and try again in two weeks. I consumed nothing but soup and water from the time I cried in the rejection room until I reentered the same space to try again a fortnight later. On the second try, I hit the lowest weight of my grown life. That July, I enlisted and immediately bought a Butterfinger and Diet Coke from the waiting room vending machine to celebrate.

Age 19, 165 lbs.

I kept the weight down through basic training until medic training, at which point the scale started to show the presence of the cafeteria next door and the effects of weekend parties in San Antonio. I failed height/weight again... by one pound. I stayed after formation to promise Drill Sergeant French I wouldn't eat anything and that he could retest me in 24 hours. He said, "That's no way to live your military career, Private. You're only a biscuit away from failure at any given moment. Let this be your warning to get some space between you and that fail." The phrase "a biscuit away" would keep me in shape until I got pregnant.

Age 20, 220 lbs.

During pregnancy number one, I took the freedom provided by the phrase "eating for two" literally. My weird craving was gas station hot dogs, and my favorite workout was to walk the two blocks from my beautiful uptown brownstone to Sebastian Joe's Ice Cream for my daily eggnog cone. In spite of these unhealthy habits, I was still stunned when, at my last prenatal appointment, the doctor told me I weighed in at 220. I had never imagined I'd pass 200 lbs. in my life! I felt huge.

Age 20.5, 170 lbs.

But also, I was twenty years old, so I lost it all in time for the big family wedding four months after having the baby. I don't think I tried at all. I just kind of rubber-banded back to where my body wanted me to be.

Age 21, 190 lbs.

I shot back up with pregnancy number two, despite trying to make better choices this time. I walked daily in the Georgia heat and limited my cravings to one gas station zebra cake per day, but even against my best efforts, I hit 220 lbs. again. After my second baby, losing it was harder. I fought to get down to 190, where I would stay for a few years.

Age 25, 169 lbs.

As my babies became toddlers, with my weight the only thing standing between me and a military promotion, I became significantly more dedicated to my weight goals. I found a wonderful personal trainer and went to the gym five times a week. I tracked all my food, got a phentermine prescription to stop the cravings, ran 5Ks, and within four months, I dropped from the 190s to the 160s again. I felt great! I passed height/weight and got compliments about how great I looked.

Age 26, 158 lbs.

During a run in my neighborhood, I passed out. I then realized I had only had two Slim Fast shakes and two eggs in the last 24-hour period. I had already been prescribed an inhaler because I was pushing myself so hard that it hurt to breathe when I ran. Smoking probably didn't help, but I heard quitting caused weight gain, and that's all I needed to know to hear to keep on puffing.

Age 27, 165 lbs.

Soon, those compliments became unwelcome advances—a random ass grab from a stranger at the bar, a van of young guys catcalling at me while I ran through my neighborhood, and a creepy higher-ranking Sergeant First Class who spiked my drink, cornered me in the clinic, and found any way possible to get me alone or touch me. The insane jealousy that oozed from my husband as he saw guys noticing me didn't help, especially when it meant he couldn't be my best friend and refuge in this scary new terrain. The running hurt my joints, eventually causing the stress fracture that turned into a full break in my right foot during that half-marathon I shouldn't have signed up for. I told myself that none of that would have happened if I was still big.

Age 28, 205 lbs.

That creepy Sergeant affected me more than I wanted to admit. The attention and issues kept piling up. I didn't like being small anymore. I left the Army, crossed back into the 200-pound range, and very much intentionally decided to be big again.

Age 31, 250 lbs.

I had developed what my therapist would call "fat armor," where I mentally used my weight as a shield against the attention and expectations I had received when I was smaller. I gained it all back so that I could become invisible again. I quickly bounced back up right past my previous highest-ever weight, 220 lbs., when I had been nine months pregnant. It was only when I dared to finally weigh myself again, as I admitted defeat in trying to lose weight for my sister's wedding, that I clocked in at 250 pounds.

Age 35 and beyond, ??? lbs.

I'm less than 250, but more than the military standard. I'm focusing on my health and nutrition through eating the right foods, taking vitamins, and drinking more water, but I can feel the fat armor looming over me. As soon as someone says in their cheeriest compliment voice, "Whoa, have you lost weight?" I go straight to McDonald's. When the clothes I've become comfortable in for the last few years start getting too big, I stop counting calories for a few days. If I catch a reflection where I think, "Damn, I look good," I start snacking at night again. I've lost the same ten pounds at least four times this year because I want to be ready, but I'm not.

I've got some mental work before I can keep it off. I need to get myself to a better head space and tell myself different stories of how it could be to live in a healthy weight range before it's going to stick. I know I can get there. I just hope it's before any health issues set in.

The Lesson: Fix Your Why

I know how to lose weight. I could probably write a book on it: calories, macros, cardio, etc. I have to be honest with myself in saying I don't know if I want to... yet. I still want to lose it eventually because I don't want diabetes and knee problems like most of the members of one side of my family or hypertension and heart disease like the other. I am learning to be content with where I am, but I truly believe there is a place where I can be both content and healthy—and I'm working on getting there.

If you're working at it, too, whether you quietly do the work every day or post your meal plans and workouts on my Instagram, I see you. My thoughts to you are for happiness and contentment, not for a number on a scale.

But if you want to "fix it," you must fix your mind first. If you have already felt it as a failure or are seeing real health consequences, and your body is failing you with bad joints, high blood pressure, or other issues, you may need to do something immediately. But if the fat armor or the craving to stay invisible is holding you back, a gym won't help, but a therapist might.

Part of igniting the change will be to gauge whether your motivation is extrinsic or intrinsic. Extrinsic motivations are the reasons that involve other people. For example, my mom commented about it, a stranger pointed at me, I don't want the embarrassment of requesting a seat belt extender on the airplane, and so on. Those are extrinsic motivators. Intrinsic ones come from within yourself, such as when I catch a candid photo or sudden reflection of myself, I feel a deep pang of not liking how I look *or* feel inside. I can tell that carrying this extra weight is taking away from my enjoyment of movement or adding to the exhaustion of just existing. Even in a hypothetical isolation chamber with no one else's thoughts in consideration, I want to change. Intrinsic motivation is the one that sticks.

So, how do you find that motivation if you really feel like it's the external factors pushing you? You ask yourself why then ask why again and again until it hurts a little.

Why do I want to weigh less than 250? To be healthy. Not just for right now but because I know that carrying too much extra weight can compound joint and heart issues for future years. While I pride myself in being more of a live-fast-die-young type, my kids deserve better than watching me slowly or painfully deteriorate into a preventative illness. But that's for later; the real question is...

Why do I want to be healthy *now*? To have more time and opportunities in my life. Did you know that at 250, I can't ride a horse on the trails in Colorado? I can't safely float in a glass bottom boat to see the bioluminescent microbes in Puerto Rico. I could miss out on some beautiful experiences because my brain is getting in the way of my body. It's silly, and the why behind being healthy is much more important than why I may get a McDouble.

So going back to my TikTok therapist, Matthias Barker, I shifted from shame-based goals to dream-based goals. My motivation to lose weight is not because I'm being chased by societal standards or fear of future unhealthiness. My motivation is dreaming of that horseback ride in the mountains or that kayak in the Caribbean. My dreams are stronger than my shame, and I'd bet yours are, too.

K.E. MACPHIE

The Fail: I Was $77,000 in Debt

My first credit card was a Flex Perks Visa. I got it as soon as I came home from basic training. I was nineteen, getting my first apartment uptown, and buying a car to replace my high school junker. Getting a credit card was the next awesome step toward being an adult, right?

I did okay with it for a while. I had a lot saved up from training and already had a job lined up, so I used new plastic money to fly around the country to visit friends at college, then paid the balance when it was due. My credit score was improving, and my airline points were adding up, so the military bank sent an offer for a $16,000 credit limit card. I figured I was just awesome and deserving of such an honor. That was 2005.

I moved to Georgia, where my husband was stationed at Ft. Stewart. Having a baby to care for and living between two deployments became expensive. While playing house, as I was doing at twenty, I bought brand-new matching nursery sets, furnished two other bedrooms, the living room, and the kitchen, and bought the best and biggest TVs, computers, gaming systems, and whatever we wanted. We were both kids ourselves, so neither of us wanted to reign in the fun. By my son's first birthday, we had maxed out the card. I hadn't even realized that we couldn't make the $150 monthly payments because when we had to before, we just paid utilities with the credit card and used cash to pay the bill. Not anymore.

The low point of that era of debt was the day I ran out of gas on our way home from church and, in my dress and kitten heels, I had to carry my baby home a mile and a half to dig into our piggy bank, then come back to buy a couple of gallons to get the car back. That made me mad enough to make a change.

When he deployed, I was dead set on digging out of that hole. We sold everything. I moved back home with two kids and lived with mom for free, putting all of his checks and mine toward the debt. We brought the debt way down and got our credit back up enough to get a house. I got a full-time job, and with two full incomes, we paid it down further, and cash flowed our move. I didn't want to make those same mistakes a second time, so lots of craigslist purchases and gradual growth left us in pretty good shape. When my husband left the military in 2008, we were 23-year-old, debt-free homeowners and everything looked great.

We coasted on that for a bit, adjusted to just one full-time income, and celebrated with a trip to Japan in 2010. Embarking on an international trip that we couldn't afford was the second spiral down the debt hole for us.

Japan launched us into a whole new YOLO mindset. Five-star hotels, crazy expensive sushi, fugu, ferries, and clothes, we bought and did whatever we wanted because when would we ever be there again?! There was no budget whatsoever, and I had no idea what we were spending (or that it all came with international fees) on our new $24,000 credit limit card. When we came home, it didn't stop. That vacation mindset was addictive. We bought the newest games when they came out and got new clothes or furniture when I was bored with our secondhand stuff because when else could we set up our lives like this? I was comparing our 20-something selves to the lifestyles and purchasing power of my older, richer mom friends and striving for the concerts, vacations, and experiences of my child-free single friends. It cost more than we made to keep up.

In addition to the regular stuff, I added a $10,000 car loan to appear equal to the other moms in the pickup line. I took $17,000 of student loans I didn't need (the Army, Pell Grant, and Indian tribe paid my tuition, but I was still loan-eligible) because all of my other student loan-ridden friends said it

148

made sense because the rates were so low, and I could defer it for years. It made sense to take the money I didn't need, right? Once those came due, I tacked on a $12,000 personal loan to make the payments on the $44,000 credit card debt we had accrued. Instead, I paid it down and used that new space on the card to rack it back up. That all happened between 2010-2013. I kept telling myself we'd start on the debt and handle it once I finished graduate school.

So, on graduation day in June 2013, I had a master's degree, a federal job with a salary of $50,000, and I finally figured out that we all owed $77,000 of debt.

The Lesson: Mindset, Minimalism & Meditation

Depression and anxiety are the number one and two mental illnesses in the United States. They arise from a blend of genetics, brain chemistry, baseline personality, and life experiences, and since some of that is out of our control, I only want to address the parts we can work to improve. Fixing a part can't fix the whole, but it can certainly help a little.

Depression comes not always from a mix-up in these steps but from forgetting where the ending is. We may have even done all the trying and failing, but we get stuck feeling it with no real vision of how to fix it and grow from it. When money (or a severe lack thereof) was the main driver behind my suicidal ideation, it was because I had aspired to become the American dream. I failed by getting in over my head in debt, and like Wile E. Coyote, it didn't hurt my ignorant bliss one bit to run off the cliff. The sting only came once I looked down to see where I was and what's about to occur. When I looked at my accounts, I felt terrible. Faced with no guidebook, plan, or anyone to talk to about what to do when it looks as if you're okay from the outside, but the debt is crushing your soul from the inside, it was very real to assume that it was the end. Being only in my twenties with my mind reiterating that I still have sixty years to live in soul-crushing pain can make suicide look like a much better fix than actually handling the issues.

It wasn't until I found people actually talking about it and offering the next steps forward from the exact obstacles I faced that they became problems to solve rather than issues to drag me down. My sister was the first to talk to me personally about her goal of becoming debt-free. She did it, and since then, I've witnessed her incredible generosity and the beautiful life she can afford. I found communities through Dave Ramsey, Suzie Orman, Tori Dunlap, and others that gave literal baby steps on how to fix such crippling debt, then what to do when you hit that goal and have room to grow. I'm still moving forward in connection with my financial maturity, but I feel at peace, and that has made all the difference.

To find a path for fixing in general, not just finances, it's really up to you to take an honest look at how you are doing in the eight dimensions I've been mentioning. Under each dimension is a present tense statement of how to live that aspect in your best self, feel free to adjust them for yourself:

Emotional: I am coping effectively with life and creating and maintaining healthy relationships with others. I am content most of the time and have coping methods planned to deal with stress when it arises.

Environmental: I have good health by occupying pleasant, stimulating environments that support well-being. My home is in good shape, my neighborhood is safe, and I can access the things I need.

Financial: I am satisfied with my current financial state and have a good outlook for its future. I don't worry about money or need more than I have for basic living expenses.

Intellectual: I know my creative abilities and am constantly given opportunities to expand my knowledge and skills. I feel challenged at work or in hobbies to create solutions and grow my experience.

Occupational: I have personal satisfaction and enrichment from the work I do. My job aligns with my big WHY and what my core values are, and I feel valued, and like I can contribute every day.

Physical: I recognize the need for physical activity, diet, sleep, and nutrition. I am able to create time in my day and space in my life to exercise. I have access to healthy food, and, barring occasional seasons of life, I am able to sleep at least seven hours a night.

Social: I have a sense of connection, belonging, and a well-developed support system. I feel comfortable going to them with my wins and leaning on them in my fails.

Spiritual: I have a concept of a greater purpose and meaning in life. Whether my belief is in God, Allah, nature, the Universe, or anything else, I know my world is one of infinity, and I am here to contribute to a greater story of the world.

It's entirely possible that you read a bunch of those and thought, "Yup, that's me!" Awesome, you're good to go in those areas. But if you are where I was at, and you read some of those and, instead, said to yourself, "Wait... Are there really people out there who can actually say that?" There are. There are real people who can actually say—and mean—many of those statements. Additionally, it's rare that someone who is 100% in one area is 0% in another. It tends to work out such that a rising tide raises all boats. If you're doing well financially, you can afford a good environment. Within that environment, you can find and connect with good, solid social networks. Within those networks, you can build good relationships, etc.

Unfortunately, the inverse is true as well. If you're constantly stressed about your marriage, money, job, or whatever, it spills over and detracts from your ability to pour any energy into the other spaces. You need to work on them all at once. It's not popular advice because it's really fucking hard. And because there is no single right way to fix everything.

The first tip for finding success when attempting to work on everything all at once is developing an awareness that you can do it all, but you can't prioritize it all. Nothing is truly important if everything is. It becomes crucial to identify specific focus areas and laser in on them for a week, a month, a quarter, or whatever you think is reasonable to establish some realistic goals for yourself. Once you've developed some new habits or hit a milestone in that area, you can let it simmer while you focus on something else. Here's how that looked for me when I found myself at the bottom of the pit:

Like in my earlier example, I recognized that if my money problems were fixed, many other areas would become easier to fix, so I started there. I signed up for Financial Peace University, a class offered by Dave Ramsey. I registered for the next local class, so I wouldn't have time to opt out. Then I started going, and I made money my focus for January. By homing in on how I was using my money, I naturally started eating better because I realized I couldn't afford to eat out all the time. I started putting more effort into my job and asking for more tasks to bring in more income, which also allowed me to give more back, making me more satisfied in that area. Even though money was my priority, those other things naturally started improving.

Maybe for you, finances are fine, but your health is suffering. You don't sleep enough, hit McDonald's four days a week, and you're a heavy smoker headed toward lung cancer. Focus on improving upon any of those habits for a month. Make a serious attempt to quit smoking. I promise it will suck for a month, but every day gets better. Then, whenever you feel confident in your new smoke-free self, break up with McDonald's or just cut it down to once a week, but be aware that you cannot replace it with smoking. Focus on improving something else when you've stopped McDonald's and are still smoke-free. Keep making similar changes and piling them on until your health feels back on track. Then when you're stronger and healthier, focus on another dimension.

The biggest key to making these changes is to give yourself grace and allow yourself to mini fail. Each time, run through a tiny version of try it, fail it, feel it, fix it, grow. Trying is just deciding what to change and making it happen. Failing it is inevitable as you sneak a quick smoke or spend money on something you didn't have on your budget. But just as we talked about earlier in the book, plan to fail—and make it a bump instead of a full stop in that plan. Allow yourself to feel the weight of that failure, be mad at yourself, disappointed in your resolve, or even sick about it for a bit. Because then, you're going to fix it.

Do your self-review to recognize why you caved, then go to the nouns. Our bad habits are almost always tied to people, places, and things—the nouns. If I was smoking, it was likely the people I was hanging out with—my smoker friends—or I was at or near a bar with a smoking area, or I was drinking or sitting around where smoking is just something to do. People, places, things. Assess, note, and fix. Review all of this quickly, then make a change for tomorrow. Keep going. You'll have a million mini-fails, so prepare for them now and know how to move past them.

A lot of debt and debt culture in America comes from a mindset of comparison, or what we call a keeping up with the Jones mentality. My generation of millennials was pushed into college, regardless of whether it was the right next step for us as individuals because we were told a degree was the only key to success. No one informed us that the crushing student loans and other debt could follow us into middle age, hold us back from owning homes or starting businesses and that there are decent jobs out there with no degree if you're willing to work. It's not fair because we were so young and impressionable, but it was part of our culture—or our parent's culture—to fit into the college archetype with our peers. We were all so convinced that we were willing to put tens of thousands of dollars on the line to fall in place.

When I was in debt, the first thing I had to do was actually look at my balances and figure out how bad it really was. It was both the easiest thing to do and the hardest. I had to look at the problem objectively, without relying on the excuses or rationalizations I had been feeding myself for so many years to stay afloat. Share the data with a friend if you need to, as having an accountability buddy is always a good idea if you can find one. I called mine my accountabili-battle buddies. We were in this battle together, and I needed them to keep me within my left and right limits when I struggled to keep on the path alone.

But the next step was to want less. So, I started a 2017 New Year's Resolution of minimalism. I read Marie Kondo and The Minimalists, watched all the documentaries and listened to the podcasts, I printed calendars of 30-day downsizing, I posted about it and tracked it, waiting for the time that it would feel like I hit that magic spark of having just enough.

I don't know when the spark hit, but I know that every time a car full of donations or a dumpster of debris left my house, I felt lighter and calmer. I didn't hug every item as I packed it away, but I did practice gratitude for the utility and the joy that my things had given me.

Meditation only strengthened that gratitude and awareness of how little I actually need. Practicing meditation is exactly that – something you have to practice. You have to be willing to suck at it for a while and give yourself a pass to be imperfect while you learn. But when you can find a solid state of mindfulness, you can let go of more things. You can be present to what serves you in the now. Thanks to present mindfulness and gratitude, I could let go of the "skinny jeans" and the things I held onto from my past. I could let go of the "just in case" extras of things, or the "hold on to it because I'll fix it one day" junk because they didn't serve me today. And when it's done right, letting go doesn't feel like loss, it feels like freedom.

Don't force meditation to the point that it pisses you off, and don't keep pushing the reduction until you feel contentment in it. Take your time to get there, do not wedge it in because this dorky book told you to do it.

STEP 5: GROW

K.E. MACPHIE

The Fail: I Dated the Same Guy a Hundred Times

I only dated the actual same guy... nine or ten times, but I've definitely dated the same *type* of guy over and over again. The truth is, I don't know how to break out of it. From high school breakups to marriage, divorce, a failed engagement, and back again, I have a type. I'll keep this review PG-13, maybe some cussing, but no sexual content.

My "type" has nothing to do with height or hairline. He has a *really* good heart deep down, but it's hidden under this tragic backstory of trauma that has callused his soft side and made him crave unconditional love. I play the role of the only one who could possibly make him better and save him from himself. He's always insanely intelligent, usually in a hands-on aspect, but the type to fail classes in high school because he was bored or because it was all so beneath him. He thinks college is for people who need to prove something, and he's too apathetic, or against the system to attend, so he thrives in blue-collar work with his hands. He's probably a borderline alcoholic, but I overlook it because we have this magical energy and chemistry, and maybe for years, I was, too. We like the same weird music, movies, or shows, and even if we don't, I'll adjust my personality to get there. He's probably ex-military or some crazy blue-collar risk-taker who lives impulsively to complement my planning-obsessed color-coding side.

My ex-husband was sweet but had a tough upbringing, then PTSD from Iraq, so he checked the box for all the components that make up my type. Since we divorced five years ago, my significant to short-lived relationships have followed similar patterns and have always ended like episodes of Sex and the City:

Navy Guy and I were on and off for two years, and I was addicted to the random interval communication model where he'd tell me we're soul mates and then disappear for a month or two.

Hipster Boo and I were always political and lifestyle opposites (right and left, extroverted and introverted, homeowner and perma-renter, babies and flying solo). Still, we made it through a tumultuous year together, watching good movies and having great sex before realizing it could go nowhere outside his Uptown brownstone.

Bearded Libertarian was too busy with side projects and odd jobs for a girlfriend.

Kevin Costner moved to Colorado.

Miles Morales wanted someone spontaneous, and my time and money didn't match that desire.

Christmas Date had some serious short-man syndrome and was prone to picking bar fights over nothing.

Flannel Man was too deep into the local band scene and lived with too many roommates.

My breaking point came in 2018 when I dated yet another tragic Iraq veteran with a lot of baggage and a tragic backstory hidden underneath puppy dog brown eyes, an easy smile, and interesting conversation. When that one blew up, I said I was done. I'm no longer dating until I can get myself unattracted to red flags.

So, I didn't date, Tinder, or look at anyone for a year.

Then, in the midst of my self-help climb out of my post-election depression, I heard Brené Brown tell a crowd that declaring yourself single for life isn't bold; it's the coward's way out. You're not stronger for quitting; you're admitting defeat and giving up. She probably said it in a somewhat nicer way, but it hit home just the same. It dawned on me that while I really was okay by myself if I were to be real, honest, and vulnerable, I'd admit that I love being in love. So, I went back into the fray.

The first guy I dated in a year, on what I told him was our "training wheels" date, was maybe the nicest, most put-together guy who has ever shown interest in me. He was in good shape, a little older than me, owned his own successful business, had normal hobbies, and did sweet little things like holding the door and putting his hand on my back or paying for the night out expecting nothing but a goodnight kiss and a bear hug. He had an ex-wife, but they were friends, had no kids, and had a sweet and loyal dog at the house he owned. He was great, wonderful, did nothing wrong... and I got bored. I have no justifiable reason to have stopped calling him, except that there were no fireworks, no butterflies, and no magical energy, so I bailed.

Then, I got discouraged again. What does it say about me if the best guys are not my type? How many great guys have put me on their crazy ex list because of my own good heart covered in emotional baggage? How many amazing guys have I been friends with over the years determined I was too much or knew I was the type to get bored with their wonderful calmness, so they didn't even take the first step toward something more?

My biggest first crush after the best guy was all butterflies and chemistry, but after a week of wonderful dates, deep conversations, and late-night texting, he said he didn't want to be a stepdad. So, he was out.

I felt myself slipping back as I went on a "get under to get over it" date with a self-admitted "crazy Marine" with all sorts of tragic backstories, but who was super into me and begged to see me again. In spite of my declaration a year and a half prior, I justified to myself that maybe this was just my type, and I needed to lean into it.

K.E. MACPHIE

The Lesson: Grow to Love Yourself First

You know, I sent this to my editor and forgot that I didn't write this chapter. As this book has been written over the last four years of dating and breakups; an engagement, and not; I only had a placeholder that said, in all caps, "WHAT THE FUCK DID I LEARN HERE?" So, not pretending I've solved this one completely, but, like the rest of this book, I can share some stuff I've learned the hard way to get where I am now.

The dating advice world is obnoxiously full of self-help-isms, one being, "you can only love someone else as much as you love yourself." I used to listen to it and roll my eyes, but thanks to living on the other side of EMDR, I'm starting to get it.

As I'm writing this book, the man I've loved for two plus years and crushed on for five before that, came home from an eleven-hour workday to give me a kiss, and immediately get to work renovating my house. I have no doubt he loves me with everything he has, even if the capacity to love that he came with started a little broken down.

He's my type as described in the fail – a Lumberjack with the most traumatic of backstories but so much love to give; a high school dropout who was still brilliant enough to build his own six-figure tree services from nothing; a country music and true crime lover who has drawn me into sad guitars and documentaries as new personailty tropes for me to take on; a blue-collar redneck who is reluctantly coming toward the sociopolitical center with me; and of course, that unexplainable, indescribable, explosive chemistry kind of love that no one else can understand.

As I'm publishing this book, not only did Lumberjack fall apart from his precariously held together unresolved trauma, but I also deeply healed myself enough to realize that I need someone who is willing to do the work to be healed, too. We are at an impasse of real love with no where to put it.

Healing has come from many directions. My favorite therapists ascribe to the Gottman Method for couples counseling. Drs. John and Judy Gottman are nationally reknowned couples' therapists who have created structures and articulated ideas of how to create healthy relationships. They have plenty of info through the Gottman Institute on their website, blogs, and books, so I'll let you dig in there while I highlight some of the things that worked for us practically.

To start with, I had to love myself enough to bring something to the table. In so many other relationships, I thought I was so lucky to have them that I'll abandon myself for them to love me more. I'll conform to what they deserve because I don't deserve anything at all. What I've learned is that when I love myself and my hobbies and attributes, it actually gives me something to glow about, something for them to admire and love about me.

So, in the very "single girl" year leading up to Lumberjack, that's what I did. I found my love in volunteer work, motorcycle riding, my job, my kids, my everything, so that dating and guys were just a fun bonus. This is one of those obnoxious dating-isms similar to "he'll come when you you're not looking." Again, eyeroll and they don't get it. The key is to shift your focus to be so busy searching for things to love about yourself that you don't have the spare time to try to search for someone else. Lumberjack came into my life at my highest point of self-love, and I still had a way to go.

Then, getting into a relationship, we both had to unlearn some healthy habits from former partners and turn to the Gottman's to teach us how to grow together. Their Seven Principles for Making Marriage Work complemented by The Four Horsemen of

Conflict have laid a foundation for us to build something better. While I'd recommend you go read their books, the overarching themes are to love with compassion.

Giving your partner the benefit of the doubt, coming to them with love and not resentment, communicating with a goal to listen rather than to be heard are game changers for healthy cohabitation possible. But to get to a place where I am willing to be the first to apologize or seek to understand his perspective, I had to get to a place where I love and value myself enough to want happiness more than I want to be right.

In my former marriage, and even early in this relationship, I would demand an apology or wait, stewing in resentment, for him to realize how badly he screwed up. I thought this was an act of self-love because I "deserved" to be treated better than this, which meant, by default, that he "deserved" to feel bad. This doesn't actually help anyone.

What I've found as I've grown, is that if I can position it, not as him versus me, but as us versus the problem, it's much easier to start the conversation softer. It's true self-love to say I deserve to be happy, and so does he. Let's figure out how to do that together.

The biggest stretch of healing came for me in an EMDR session where I confronted my first boyfriend, the one who trained me to lower the bar.

He would tell me he loved me when it was just us, and the very next day, ignore me in the hallways, laugh at me with his friends, or act like he didn't know me if I made eye contact. So, I revisited that relationship in an EMDR session.

In the session, I brought my mind back to our high school auditorium. I don't remember what the assembly or pep rally was about, but I remember trying to say hi to this boyfriend, who said he loved me in the bench seat of his pickup the night before, and completely ignored me in front of his wrestler buddies and the cheerleaders he was trying to impress. In the actual version, I was hurt, but I left him alone and watched him from a few bleachers back in sadness, confusion, and heartbreak, but would continue to accept this shitty love from him for years to come.

The reprocessed version healed my heart.

When my adult consciousness could reenter my teen self, she stopped him after the assembly and asked if they could talk privately. They went to a side hallway, and she told him, "I do not tolerate this. The way you are treating me is not OK, but you're not capable of anything else right now, so I'm not going to ask you to change. You are incapable of the love I deserve; I just wanted you to know to your face that this really felt awful. If you ever loved me, let me go."

I don't know if their relationship ended in this alternate reality, but I know something changed in my brain. It's like I took a wrong turn twenty years ago, but I finally found my way back and took the right one. And now I'm on a path where I don't accept love like that, I don't believe I deserve to be a secret for weak men to selectively love, and the potential of what love can be has exploded to a new level of healthy reciprocity for the big love I know I am capable of giving.

The Fail: I Didn't Get the Job

I went to a job interview for a start-up healthcare company with a mission I firmly believed in and an atmosphere where I would thrive. I had a phone interview with HR, followed by two more phone interviews, after which I was invited to meet three people at the office for an afternoon. I loved it. I killed the interview, enjoyed all the people I met, and had an answer to every question and a follow-up for every idea. I even liked waiting in the beautiful light-filled exposed brick conference room as I sat feeling super confident about the whole thing.

A week later, I got an email that HR had made a decision, and they would call me the next day. I was expecting good news. If it had been bad, they would have just said so in the email, right? I started prepping my salary negotiation strategy, researched my lower limits and upper expectations, and talked to my sister and my friends about it. I was daydreaming about how my life could change with a $20,000 raise, which wasn't even considering the improved healthcare benefits and matching 401K the company offered. I was pumped and smiling when HR called me at 10:30 AM on the dot.

The woman informed me that they loved my interview but had decided to go with someone else. The hiring manager said he thought I would be a great fit for the company, but not in analytics, and that I should apply for the job in appeals and grievances instead. You know, the part of healthcare where you just get yelled at and hear sob stories all day. Fun. It's still fuzzy because I felt so shell-shocked by the rejection, but the HR rep said she would follow up with me regarding the other jobs. I never heard back.

I got off the call, and I cried. I found a reason to leave work for a bit and cry in my car before getting myself together and heading back in. I know rejection hurts no matter what, but in this case, I think it's because I don't know what went wrong. I've been in interviews where I knew it wouldn't work; I had a bad feeling, or I could tell by question four that I was underqualified. But this one felt so good.

So, I started imagining why they wouldn't hire me. Did I say something wrong? Was my $100 outfit the wrong look for their culture? Did my once-a-year makeup routine show that I was trying too hard? Was it because I was five years older or eighty pounds heavier than the girls who would be my bosses? Am I not as smart, funny, or likable as I thought I came across? Am I like that all the time? I obsessed over what was wrong with me.

The last time I didn't get a job I wanted was when I went for a state lead—my first go at it, two years before they eventually hired me. The first boss had quit abruptly, leaving the rest of the team and me holding the bag. I took the opportunity to shine in my leadership and keep things afloat. I went to every meeting and was present on every conference call. I killed it in the interview and almost sacrificed a friendship going head-to-head with my coworker for the position.

I hadn't heard a decision yet when I was sitting in yet another meeting, and the Lieutenant Colonel casually said, "Sorry to hear you missed out on the promotion. I didn't know the captain was going for the job, did you?" My face must have explained that I did not. My friend, a former military counterpart, had heard about my boss quitting and swooped in to apply for the job, knowing I was, without telling me. It was a rejection and a betrayal in one.

He stayed on for less than a year. He fudged our numbers, created animosity on the team, and made things look good for higher headquarters. When I ultimately got the role after his departure, I spent my first year in the role cleaning up. I ended up bringing Minnesota to the top five performers in the nation, but

176

I got the job because of a contract change, so I'll always know that no matter how well I did and how much progress I made, I was never their first choice.

Another job rejection I still remember was when I applied during the government furlough to work at Blue Zones for a role way beyond anything I thought I could do. It came down to me against a VP from a big Minneapolis consulting firm, and our final interview was a presentation about ourselves to the board. I was a PowerPoint wizard, so I made an awesome slide deck (kind of cringy by today's standards), and—I will forever kick myself for this—note cards. Back then, I thought all professional speakers walked around with note cards.

When I didn't get the job, they told me I did a heck of a presentation, but the hiring manager said, "The looming question in the room was, 'Who needs notecards about themselves?' Get some confidence, work on your skills, and maybe we'll see you back here someday." Not there yet, I guess.

So now, I follow my own advice. I tried it; I failed. If they call me, I'll try again, I guess. Until then, I'm going to feel bad for a bit, then work to fix my insecurities and issues and grow in preparation for something even better that I know will come soon enough.

The Lesson: If It's Meant to Be, It'll Come to Me

I found a mantra on TikTok that has given me peace in many scenarios since the stress of the COVID times took over:

If it's meant to be, it will come to me.

Trying to force a bad fit, whether in a job, with people, or with activities, is painful. It leads to little more than a profound sense of rejection, questioning yourself, negative self-talk, and feeling like a constant failure. It's much less of a failure to have built up enough self-awareness to say, "This isn't for me," and walk away.

Whenever I was rejected by a job, guy, friend, or anyone or anything else, I would contort myself to fit what I thought I wanted or distort them into something they're not. But now, I remember that I only want people and things in my life that want me,

178

too. So, if the job rejects me, it's not for me. No matter how much I romanticized it or believed that it had the potential to be perfect, it wasn't right for me at that time.

Now, years after that job rejection, I have my real dream job. I'm doing something I didn't even know existed back then, which is a culmination of everything I've been working toward during my career in public health. Not only was it an actual fit to my skills, but they wanted me to bad, they competed with another organization that wanted me to. They called and bargained and, after consulting my mom and the Chaplain on what I should do, they jumped for joy at my acceptance. With time and perspective, you find that the dream you missed out on wasn't even big enough, and if you keep going, you'll find the thing you want even more that wants you back.

I would apply this to dating. When you go over the pros and cons of a potential partner, and one of the cons is "he doesn't love me back," then it's all you need to know. That's the con that supersedes all the pros. If someone doesn't want you, you can't force it. And if you do, it won't ever feel like a good win. I wondered, since my days of hearing the Genie tell Aladdin the rules of what he won't do, why "I can't make anybody fall in love with anybody else" was on there. Now I know, even a magic cartoon Genie knows, this is something too special to force.

There's no amount of magic or wishing that can create the unique intention of something that is meant to be. The sooner you can accept that, the sooner you can grow in happiness and gratitude for the things you have instead of pining for the things you don't.

I'd love for you to find your own mantra or affirmation. In a world that tells you to "go out and take what's yours" I think we'd all be better off if we followed something like:

> I don't chase.
>
> I attract.
>
> What's meant to be
>
> Will find me.

Say it until you believe it. Say it when you're sad, when you're desperate, when you're begging the universe to give you what you want. The thing you want isn't always the thing you need. Stand firm in who you are and the things you need will make their way to you.

I'm grateful for those job losses. I learned and grew from them enough to be offered two dream jobs where I picked one. And I still believe this dream job will reveal an even bigger purpose for me in the future. Maybe it will be a direct line to a bigger career path, maybe it will help me meet someone who can expand my worldview, or maybe it just gives me the peace and space to grow as an author or a speaker. I couldn't write this book if I were still working three jobs, stressed about money, and sad about life. What has made this job such a dream is that it has given me space – financially, emotionally, intellectually, fiscally – to have the capacity to continue to grow outside of it.

The Fail: I Wanted to Die... But I Haven't Yet

** CONTENT WARNING: For this chapter: this is going to outline some dark thoughts and detailed plans for suicide (asterisks will indicate where to start and stop reading) **

--

I haven't told anyone this for an odd reason. I have been worried for years that if I made it public, I wouldn't have the option to go for it if I ever felt like I needed to again. But it's suicide awareness month, and this is me officially letting go and leaving it behind.

It also gets into some of what helped and got me out after and what you can do if you find yourself on either end of it.

182

Four years ago, from about November 2015 through January 2016, was the peak of many of the failures I've outlined in this book. I was at, or near, my highest weight and felt it. My ex-husband had just moved back to Minnesota and seeing him was infuriating (I remember why we divorced) and conflicting (I still cared about him and questioned if I had made the right call months before). I had been dumped by the most significant boyfriend of my life (and it wouldn't be the last time, but this time Adele's album, *25*, had just come out and set the soundtrack to it all). I had to leave my therapist because we learned she wasn't in-network after $900 of visits I couldn't afford. The kids were struggling in school and sanity. I was missing my sisters, who moved hundreds of miles from our hometown as I had always dreamed I would. I had missed out on a promotion. I was donating plasma to tread water on the bills, and tens of thousands of dollars of debt suffocated me. It was a lot.

The tipping point came when I called one of many debt collectors, and they said they could lower my minimum payment if I filled out a monthly finance form to find out where I had space to pay them. I did the form honestly and sent it back, and the collector on the other end said with sadness in his voice, "Ma'am, according to this, your basic bills are more than you make. We can't work with you without space to make reasonable payments. We'll have to keep the payments as-is."

That was it. I couldn't even take small steps to improve my circumstances, so it would never get better. And even if it DID get better, I was fighting like hell to move from drowning to struggling. What a pathetic thing to want to look forward to, I told myself.

** STOP reading here if a plan of suicide would be triggering in your current space. **

I was in a cycle of still showing up in life to fulfill my responsibilities. I made it to work and took the kids to theater or basketball. I know some forms of depression aren't so active, but otherwise, I would just lay awake in bed. I was always in bed but never asleep. This bizarre insomnia was enough to get me to the doctor for sleeping pills, but I was careful not to let on to her about the depression. I deliberately didn't check the blocks that said, "Have you felt hopeless in the last six months?" because I knew she might not give me the pills. I needed those to start the plan.

After a suicide, people wonder what that happy friend with so much ahead of them could have been thinking. Well, I'll tell you: The rationalization started with the ex-husband bonding again with the kids while I hid in my room. I could die, and they would be okay. They would be better than okay because my life insurance would pay off the debt, my ex-husband would be happy to stay in the house and have the kids full-time, and my ex-boyfriend would feel like a jerk and regret losing me forever (okay, that was a petty justification, but whatever, it existed).

The biggest lie I told myself was that I had already screwed up my kids so badly that at least having a dead parent would allow them some pity in the world for how terrible they would inevitably turn out. These beliefs felt as true as the laws of gravity to my depressed mind. Yeah, sure, I knew people would be sad, but they would get over it. They'd cry for a while, but then they wouldn't. People are resilient.

The key was to make it look like an accident, not a suicide. I couldn't let my kids think I chose to leave them, just that it was my time to go. So, I had a plan. We had a great snowy Saturday together one day in January, and I knew Sunday would be a good time to do it. I told them I had to run some errands while planning never to see them again. They gave me a quick "Bye, mom" while glued to Mario Kart on the TV. I put the sleeping pills in my purse and got in the car. I was going to take enough to show up in a toxicology test, then crash my car somewhere isolated to be sure no one else was hurt, but where it would be found soon—something like driving into a tree or off a freeway ramp. I had a few locations in mind, but I drove east, cried, and listened to Radiohead while I tried to find the courage to do it.

START reading again to hear how I healed those triggering thoughts.

I wandered and drove until I crossed one of the bridges on my list and ended up at my grandma's cemetery. The last time I had been there was the day I filed for divorce a year earlier. It's a God spot of mine, somewhere in the world I can go and feel a little closer to God, a place I feel more spiritual than normal. I remember getting out and the biting cold air hurting my face where I had been crying. I got to her spot, laid down on the cold ground, and cried. I asked her to help me. I said out loud to the snowy tombstone, "I just don't know what else I can do."

I can't adequately describe the feeling that overcame me, but it was a warmth and pressure— almost like a hug or being wrapped in a heavy blanket. My tears stopped. My mind cleared. And it wasn't a voice, but a distinct feeling that someone told me it would get better. I laid there a while longer, then got in my car and went home. I wouldn't toss the pills for another year, but I never attempted the plan again.

--

** If you or someone you know is experiencing suicidal thoughts or a crisis, please reach out immediately and call or text the Suicide Prevention Lifeline at **988**, Veterans, press 1. These services are free and confidential. **

The Lesson: Give Yourself a Future to Grow Into

I was first suicidal when I was fifteen. At the time, emo culture was a thing, so maybe it wasn't real, or perhaps a "cry for attention," but it wasn't recognized as anything real or valid for very long. I would cut my wrists and tell my sisters that the cat did it. I once took a bunch of Tylenol but only got a stomachache, which only made me more pissed than I had been when I thought it could kill me.

Weird things stopped me from actually doing it. One was triggered by the idea that I had braces in my mouth that mom had already paid half for, so she'd be out $2,000 just to have to see an ugly metal mouth at the wake. So, I decided not to kill myself while I still had braces. It sounds silly now, but what can I say? It totally saved my life a couple of times.

Another was a poem I found on Tumblr that was a reshare of an old PostSecret, both staples of emo communities back then:

> *Fuck the poets of the past, my friends.*
> *There are no beautiful suicides. Just*
> *cold corpses with shit in their pants*
> *and the end of their gifts.*

By the time the braces came off, I had grown into a happier and more confident person and wasn't suicidal anymore. I still had strong emotions but didn't feel the pull to kill myself for another eleven years.

So other than the spirit of my deceased grandmother or braces or a blog post, what else helped me that could possibly help your suicidal friend? Most of you probably have no idea how bad I felt, but many people knew I wasn't well. I think the key is just to show up and offer support however you do it best. Be there.

My mom would pick me up, buy me dinner, and talk. I didn't talk much back, and due to her nonconfrontational Catholic upbringing, she's not one to directly confront me with questions like, "Do you want to kill yourself?" but she could tell I needed to get out of my house, and she had the means to pull me out and make me exist for a few hours.

My sisters made more trips home, texted funny emojis, or called when I went too long without responding. Again, not asking it outright, but telling me they loved me, and they cared whenever they could.

My friend, Adeana, let me walk in whenever and cry on her couch. She made good food and had the same sense of humor, which she could use to pull me out of a rut. I'd show up puffy-faced and word-vomiting about whichever of the above problems was surfacing, and she just listened and empathized. I started coming out of my suicidal mental cancer just as she discovered her very real breast cancer, and I realized that her being there for me showed me how to be a good friend to her when she needed it, and I got to return the favor through months of chemo and couch talks for her.

My work friend could feel it as if he had a 6th sense. He'd buy me a beer at happy hour to let me vent, offer to fix my car for free, or cover my work and let me cut out early. He defended me to the new boss, saying, "She's not normally like this, be patient."

Show up how you can. If you're the funny friend, be funny. If you have extra money, treat your friend or send them an anonymous gift. If you can give them some regular time, like a Thursday girls' night or monthly book club, keep inviting them. Give your sad friend an easy invite, something where they feel like they're not putting you out. Stick it out because they might also avoid you and not call you back, so it means a lot if you're still there when they start climbing out. Don't take it personally; they hate themselves, not you.

The other thing that helped immensely was giving myself dream-based goals. Having lost the election, I also faced the loss of an entire vision of the future—both my next year and the rest of my life—so I had to re-picture it. I began by setting tiny goals I would aim to achieve in place of that future that no longer existed. I chose to travel and booked a local trip for the upcoming May. I looked up Airbnb's, calculated mileage, and researched what I would do once I got there. Once I had a couple of pieces of the puzzle put together, I could see there might still be more I could do. It helped a lot.

And what do you do if you're me? Say you're a person who has been suicidal on and off since you were fifteen or so. It comes at some obvious low points and unexpectedly at random times. Suicide feels like a constant plan Z, for if nothing else works. So, what are the things that have kept me further from that point, even through the rough spots since?

- a list of my God spots that I go to when I feel myself nearing the edge

- writing and oversharing to help sort things out for me

- avoiding alcohol - it makes me feel better until you feel much, much worse

- having something to look forward to - a trip, a budget, or a 1- or 5-year-plan

- suicide prevention training from professionals

- a good therapist, and specifically, diving into EMDR to do some deep healing

- a dog or something fuzzy to love you unconditionally

The biggest insight I can share is to stop thinking that you will be cured. Maybe you won't. This is your brain. It's your life. Accept it now and learn to manage it. Understanding that has helped free me from the constant burning need to solve it, and instead, it allows me to tell myself, "This is going to come again, and next time I'll be ready. I need to feel it before I can fix it, but I will always come out the other side."

When I lost the election, three years after my lowest low, I felt the depression and the suicidal signs creeping in, but I opted to allow myself to feel sad and live in it, knowing it would get better. And that's exactly what happened. And that's what will happen next time. I'm going to get sad again someday, but while I'm not, I can get myself the people, the tools, and the plans prepared and accessible to pull out when it hits. The thoughts don't come as easily as they used to. I'm getting stronger. You can, too.

In my motivation workshop with Matthias Barker, he did a life-changing meditation that I still lean on today:

At one of his workshops in 2022, we "met" two of our five-year future selves in a meditation – one if we stuck to all the goals and good habits we set, one if we did not. Like *A Christmas Carol,* but with fewer Muppets.

In meeting the one who did not, I had to go outside to find her. I walked through my kitchen and there she was outside in the dark, hunched over and chain smoking on the back patio. She was drunk and glared at me with hateful eyes and deep wrinkles that served as the scars of sadness for so many years on her face. She didn't talk much, but I could sense a loss and a hopelessness in her. My present-day self could only slightly console her and tell her she's doing her best, and I'm sorry. And then I left.

Back in my living room, I manifested my positive five-year future self: the one who changed her habits and moved toward the life I was dreaming of. She came into the room confidently and sat near me. She looked…. content. She wasn't skinny, but she was strong, and her clothes fit perfectly on her. She wasn't obnoxiously optimistic, just positive and self-assured. She smiled warmly through our conversation, and she ended with the same things I told my sad self: she was proud of me for doing my best.

Seeing a clear vision of the outcomes of my dream-based goals created a framework to make my life better. Every decision – to stop medicated weight loss, start cooking, quit smoking, learning when to be the first to apologize after a fight, everything – has been because it's what I think she would have done. And I'm absolutely better for it.

I would highly suggest you try it, through meditation or even more consciously through just writing it out or thinking out loud. All I want, the whole sum of this book, is that I wish for the best life for everyone, I'm just offering one way to help you see it.

When we did the same meditation at the January 2023 workshop, a year later, the same positive self came back, but instead of walking in the room with a gentle self-assuredness, she came *running* in like she was bursting with excitement and said, "YOU'RE DOING IT! I'm so proud of you!" I cried and thanked her profusely because I knew she was right. I'm on the right path, and this book, this hope to lead the way for friends and strangers, is just one more step in that direction.

It's not always easy, and I know a lot of what I've said sounds out there or maybe far away from where you feel, but it's just one path of many and this is just a place to share everything I've learned along the way.

If you need help getting there, always know you can reach out to me. If you're feeling it now or if you can see it coming like a storm on the horizon,

I'm here for you.

I've been in that pit, and I know the way out.

Sources, Inspiration, and Recommended Reading

Barker, M. (2023) *Matthias J Barker*. Available at: https://matthiasjbarker.com/ (Accessed: January 14, 2023).

Brown, B. (2010) *The Gifts of Imperfection: Letting Go of Who You Think You're Supposed to Be and Embrace Who You Are.* Center City: Hazelden Publishing.

Brown, B. (2012) *Daring Greatly: How the Courage to be Vulnerable Transforms the Way We Live, Love, Parent, and Lead.* New York City: Gotham

Brown, B. (2015) *Rising Strong: The Reckoning, the Rumble, the Revolution.* New York: Random House.

Brown, B. (2017) *Braving the Wilderness: The Quest for True Belonging and the Courage to Stand Alone.* New York: Random House

Brown, B. (2021) *Atlas of the Heart.* New York: Random House.

Department of Health and Human Services (2016) *Creating a Healthier Life: A Step-By-Step Guide to Wellness | SAMHSA Publications and Digital Products.* Available at: https://store.samhsa.gov/product/Creating-a-Healthier-Life/SMA16-4958 (Accessed: January 14, 2023).

Duckworth, A. (2019) *Grit.* London: Vermilion.

Fields Millburn, J., Nicodemus, R. (2011) *Minimalism: Live a Meaningful Life.* Missoula: Asymmetrical Press.

Gottman, J. (1999) *The Seven Principles for Making Marriage Work.* New York: Three Rivers Press

Harris, D. (2014) *10% Happier: How I Tamed the Voice in My Head, Reduced Stress Without Losing My Edge, and Found Self-Help That Actually Works.* New York: HarperCollins

Hoff, B. (1982) *The Tao of Pooh.* Boston: Dutton Books.

Hyatt, M. (2019) *Your Best Year Ever.* Mumbai: Embassy Books.

Kondo, M. (2014) *The Life-Changing Magic of Tidying Up: The Japanese Art of Decluttering and Organizing.* Berkeley: Ten Speed Press.

Loscalzo J. A celebration of failure. Circulation. 2014 Mar 4;129(9):953-5. doi: 10.1161/CIRCULATIONAHA.114.009220. PMID: 24589694; PMCID: PMC3974547.

Menakem, R. (2017). *My Grandmother's Hands.* Las Vegas: Central Recovery Press

Newport, C. (2019) *Digital Minimalism: Choosing a Focused Life in a Noisy World.* New York: Portfolio

Pirsig, R. (1974) *Zen and the Art of Motorcycle Maintenance.* New York: William Morrow

Ramsey, D. (2007) *Total Money Makeover.* Nashville: Nelson Books.

Sandage SA. *Born Losers: A History of Failure in America.* Harvard University Press; Cambridge, MA: 2005.

Tough P. What if the secret to success is failure? *NY Times.* 2011 Sep 14

Sincero, J. (2013) *You Are a Badass: How to Stop Doubting Your Greatness and Start Living an Awesome Life.* Philadelphia: Running Press

Sinek, S. (2009) *Start with Why: How Great Leaders Inspire Everyone to Take Action*. London: Portfolio Penguin.

Sinek, S. (2014) *Leaders Eat Last: Why Some Teams Pull Together and Others Don't*. New York: Portfolio/Penguin

Sinek, S. (2017) *Find Your Why: A Practical Guide for Discovering Purpose for You and Your Team*. New York: Portfolio/Penguin

Van der Kolk, B. (2014), *The Body Keeps Score: Brain, Mind, and Body in the Healing of Trauma*. New York: Penguin.

Wiest, B. (2020) *The Mountain is You*. New York: Thought Catalog Books

About the Author

Kirsten has started a dozen stories on paper and in her laptop, but this is her first published book.

When she's not writing, she is parenting teenagers, fostering animals, public health-ing as a domestic violence preventionist, selling houses as a Realtor, reading a lot of books, riding her motorcycle, traveling anywhere, listening to alt-chic rock, or just relaxing at home with her Lumberjack in the Twin Cities or in the Northwoods of Minnesota.

To learn more about Kirsten, or to see other fails and photos to go along with them, visit failinggood.com.

K.E. MACPHIE, LLC

Made in the USA
Monee, IL
17 August 2023

41186278R00115